"If thinking differently has ever gotten you in trouble or had you feeling like you don't fit in, this book is a must-read.

Think Possible will help you turn your biggest struggle—thinking differently—into your superpower. And it will help you hone your superpower like a laser beam, to effect massive change in the world.

Allison Garner spent 20 years as a chemical engineer in the oil industry and as vice president of an engineering consulting firm. She was a maverick—a highly successful woman leader in a male-dominated field.

She's spent her life busting down walls and breaking out of boxes. Now she's going to share with you how thinking outside the box, can help you create a life of leadership and impact."

RICH LITVIN,
Founder of 4PC and Co-author of *The Prosperous Coach*

"Allison Garner takes you on her intensely personal journey on how she overcomes the barriers that hold most of us back, both professionally and personally. She has a gift for breaking down complex issues through engaging storytelling and self-reflection to give you very practical guidance for self-improvement. Allison is a well-respected community leader who practices the techniques that she presents in her civic life."

ANDREW LEAVITT,
Chancellor, University of Wisconsin - Oshkosh

"Allison Garner is a proven leader in my community. She is not afraid to make tough decisions and has the wisdom and tenacity to help guide our community forward. The chapter that most resonated with me is when she addresses psychological safety. This will help me build a better team in my business, which is in the creative industry, and one has to be allowed to take risks without fear of retribution. If you lead a team of any kind, you need to read this book."

DIANE PENZENSTADLER,
Owner of 44° North Advertising & Design,
2018 Governor's Trailblazer Award Recipient for Women in Business

"*Think Possible* is like having a 1-1 conversation with Allison Garner and reflects her beliefs and values. Four words that come to mind in describing Allison are honest, genuine, authentic, and reflective. Those same words could describe *Think Possible*. I have known Allison for about seven years when we both served on an advisory board for a charter school her children attended. I have experienced her skills in action in facilitating meetings and conversations by her asking great questions causing others to reflect and make discoveries, to see other viewpoints, and to reach better and more innovative solutions. She is an active listener with an uncanny ability to summarize viewpoints and help others stretch their thinking and their confidence to think outside the box. *Think Possible* will encourage and challenge me to hone my own leadership and facilitation skills in my journey of continuous improvement as a servant leader. I encourage others to read and internalize Allison's ideas to grow personally and professionally."

DR. BARB HERZOG, PHD,
School Board President, retired Deputy Superintendent

"*Think Possible* is like sitting down with a funny, straight-talking friend who gives you practical tools to go from good to great. Master coach, Allison Garner, has distilled much of her coaching know-how into this practical and inspiring book. World-class leaders self-reflect—because all true leadership comes from within. If you are ready to debunk your excuses and to take your life and leadership to the next level, you need this book."

DR. MANDY LEHTO, PhD,
Coach, Speaker, Writer

"This book encourages leaders to re-consider their perspectives on the role that fear has on the decision-making process. Leaders are often trained to follow the lonely road of acting decisive, businesslike, and 'staying the course'. This approach, however, falls short in many situations. By demonstrating a level of openness, empathy, and considering the upsides of alternative unproven scenarios, we can often be led to more humanized, engaged outcomes as well as greater satisfaction and value. The book's presentation about thinking differently has led me to take pause about the meaning of my work, the relationships I have with my tribes, and whether 'service' and 'ego-serving' are complementary aims. Allison's anecdotes lead readers to immediately want to apply offered ideas to their own life experiences."

JASON WHITE,
President & CEO,
Greater Oshkosh Economic Development Corporation

THINK
POSSIBLE

THINK POSSIBLE

The Light and Dark Side of Never Running Out Of Ideas

ALLISON GARNER

NEW YORK

LONDON • NASHVILLE • MELBOURNE • VANCOUVER

Think Possible

© 2019 Allison Garner

Published in New York, New York, by Morgan James Publishing. Morgan James is a trademark of Morgan James, LLC. www.MorganJamesPublishing.com

The Morgan James Speakers Group can bring authors to your live event. For more information or to book an event visit The Morgan James Speakers Group at www.TheMorganJamesSpeakersGroup.com.

ISBN 978-1-64279-073-3 paperback
ISBN 978-1-64279-074-0 eBook
Library of Congress Control Number: 2018942761

Cover Design by:
Rachel Lopez
r2c design
www.r2cdesign.com

Interior Design by:
Megan Whitney Dillon
Creative Ninja Designs
megan@creativeninjadesigns.com

In an effort to support local communities, raise awareness and funds, Morgan James Publishing donates a percentage of all book sales for the life of each book to Habitat for Humanity Peninsula and Greater Williamsburg.

Get involved today! Visit
www.MorganJamesBuilds.com

CONTENTS

INTRODUCTION

I t was the fifth day of working in London. I was staying in a part of the city that was crowded, loud and a concrete jungle. After joining the throngs of professionals making their way to their places of business each day, I was becoming sick of the noises, smells, sounds, and sights of the city. My poor, small town brain was having input overload. There were few trees, no grass and the river was a milky shade of brown. My inner child was yearning for a field of flowers or a pristine lakeside path. Because we had the day off, I agreed to join my colleagues for some obligatory sightseeing. We carted ourselves across town, shuttling through the Underground stations and emerged near Westminster Abbey.

We walked and gawked and gazed and took photos. We oohed over the architecture. We aahed over the history. Then we came upon a quaint little park hidden from the hustle and bustle of the city. I was being drawn to the park as if an invisible force were leading me there on a leash. There was grass, like the green stuff that grows out of the ground. It was glorious! There were trees and flowers and birds and the sound of the wind tickling the leaves.

We lay in the grass. The sun, which doesn't seem to come out much in London, was shining brightly. I could almost feel my Vitamin D and serotonin levels surge. The grass underneath my body was soft and soothing. The hot, brilliant sun on my face was exquisite. As if things couldn't get any better, I felt a warm, wet tongue on my face. When I opened my eyes, I was greeted by a very friendly beagle who was eagerly covering me in kisses and wagging his tail. It was in this moment that I felt beautiful, loved, vulnerable, authentic and perfect.

It was on the 10th day of working in London that I experienced another moment of authenticity, vulnerability and complete willingness to allow for love and belonging. There were about 30 of us professional coaches who were in a mastermind group together. As coaches, we are always working to grow and develop ourselves, and the work is intense. My ego doesn't like it when my coaching colleagues tell me to lean into my edge. However, I chose to ignore that voice and do the scary thing.

As I sat looking at all my fellow coaches, I asked them to see my heart. It was an edgy ask for me, since my default is to be in my mind snuggled up cozily with my ego. By choosing to be in my heart, I was choosing a different pathway. And when I asked, I did the thing that I have been avoiding most of my life. I cried as every person in the room looked at me. I chose to stay in that moment. To allow it to happen. To do the thing I NEVER do. And when I looked up, I saw the person across from me showing me her love by looking into my tear-filled eyes and meeting my gaze. When I looked at the person next to her, he did the same thing. And on and on around the room I went, meeting each person's gaze and soaking up their love for me. It was intense, humbling, energizing and life-changing.

These two experiences from London taught me that being truly present is so much more powerful than being stuck inside my head, which is full of to-do lists, stories and memories. My mind is the thing that tells me to do, to be in action, to keep busy, to finish one more thing.

When I can drop into my body, I experience peace and calm, I can hear things that aren't even being said, I can feel things that cannot be seen. My mind is like my sister-in-law's schnauzer (may he rest in peace) where you could literally wind him in circles by twirling his nubby tail around your finger. When you stopped winding him, he'd have to unwind himself by spinning in the opposite direction. By dropping into my body, my mind doesn't spin me around in circles.

I've been the person who believed very deeply that "doing" was the answer. If something needed doing, then I was your girl. I loved the feeling of crossing items off my list, of being busy, of being on the go, of feeling important and needed. I now realize this behavior prevented me from knowing myself, which was really handy since I didn't really like who I was. It also allowed my ego to run roughshod over me, which resulted in a lot of emotional pain and misery.

All of this is to say that as I ran from who I am, a person who thinks differently from everyone else in the room, I let my ego and my mind run my life. When I stopped running and let my heart lead the way, I discovered the thing I'd been running from was actually an enormous superpower. I started to use my gift. I had impact. I changed lives. I became unstoppable.

My clients are me. They think differently. They may be compulsive doers. They may be hiding who they are. They may not feel like they belong. They may not be truly present. They may not even know what I mean when I say dropping into my body. They may be chock full of big, bold ideas ready for launch but let the ego dismiss these ideas as foolish or impossible. And I walk that journey with them, drawing out their strengths, upleveling their mission and acknowledging who they ARE in the world. They are having big impact. They are changing lives. They are unstoppable too. This book is about them, about me and about you.

CHAPTER ONE.
YOUR TRIBE IS EVERYTHING

"Set your life on fire. Seek those who fan your flames"

RUMI

The term "tribe" is commonly used to describe a closely connected group of people who look out for each other. Our human-ness makes us yearn to belong to a tribe. For thousands of years, we have depended on our tribes for everything. It seems ironic to me that in an era when all of us can connect more easily than ever that we are more disconnected and disengaged than ever. This impacts our tribes. While it may be easier to form a tribe given the ease of communicating using technology, many of us have no tribe at all. Instead, we have loads of acquaintances, online "friends" and professional connections whom we interact with in an ongoing cycle of observing them, then reacting to them, more than we ever truly connect with them. But these are not the same as a tribe. Members of a tribe are committed to each person's best interests.

Average of Five

It is said that you are the average of the five people with whom you spend the most time. If this is true, then your tribe really does matter. If I choose to spend most of my time with people who gossip, make snap judgments about others and focus on negative energy, then I will most likely gossip, judge and think negatively, whether I do it sub-consciously or not, I've been inhabited by my surroundings. By the way, I've personally run this experiment and found it to be true.

I met a therapist who explained to me the theory of the "average of five" on a white board, which really appealed to my engineering self who loves white boards and formulas and charts. She asked for the names of my five closest friends which she wrote on the board. She asked if each of these friends gave more to me or took more from me. If they took more, they got a negative sign. If they gave more, they got a positive sign. Then she asked how each friend would rank on a scale of 1 to 10, 1 being low and 10 being high, in terms of how much they give or take. Here is an example of how this might look:

Bob	Sue	Fred	Mary	Tom
+	-	-	+	+
5	3	1	8	9

The next step was to add up the positive and negative scores and divide the total by 5.

$$5 + -3 + -1 + 8 + 9 = 18$$

$$18 / 5 = 3.6$$

If you have an average score of -10 to 0, then you are not being supported by your people. This will impact your ability to weather difficult storms, do amazing work and build your self-confidence. If your score is 0.1 to 4.0, then you have some good supports, but not enough to truly fill you up. There are still too many low scorers in your circle. If your score is 4.1 to 7.0, then your tribe has people who are high quality supports which means they can give you more than they take from you. These people contribute to keep you emotionally, mentally and spiritually in alignment with your inherent potential. If your average score is 7.1 to 10.0, then you are the poster child for how to surround yourself with people who truly empower and energize you. You have a very high-quality tribe.

The higher the score, the more your friends fill you up and the more likely it is that you can manage the ups and downs of life, continue to grow, develop an evolved consciousness and be *amazing*. By evaluating each friendship separately, you can easily spot where improvements can be made.

Recognizing how a tribe can support and uplift you is how you may come to outgrow some friendships while nourishing others. Your tribe is the place where you can take your mask off when everyone is watching and be yourself. They will accept you for who you are. They may even see a more remarkable and stunning you and inspire you to become that. They will stand beside you when you are scared, hold you up when you are tired, cheer you on when you are in battle and be a soft place to land when life gets tough. They are critical to your wellbeing, so it's best to make sure they are the right people for you.

Psychological Safety

Amy Edmundson coined the term "psychological safety" after studying nursing teams in hospitals. Her PhD thesis was that cohesive teams would report less errors, but the data came back with the opposite result. Her study found that the more cohesive the team, the higher the number of reported errors. She went back to the data and poured over it to find how this could be. She discovered the more cohesive teams were much less fearful of reporting their mistakes, thereby resulting in a higher rate of *reporting* errors. Psychological safety within a team allows us to admit when we don't know something and tell people when we've made a mistake. It's when we feel safe to be vulnerable, and it makes for a really powerful team.

In 2012, Google launched Project Aristotle to define the characteristics of a highly productive team. One of the findings was that psychological safety was critical for the teams that soared. Google was kind enough to create a simplified checklist of how to create psychological safety so the rest of us mortals can do it too. Charles Duhigg, who wrote, Smarter Faster Better, provides Google's checklist.

1. Do not interrupt teammates during conversations.

2. Demonstrate listening by summarizing what people say after they say it.

3. Admit what they don't know.

4. Before ending a meeting, ensure that all team members have spoken at least once.

5. Encourage people who are upset to express their frustrations, and encourage teammates to respond in nonjudgmental ways.

6. Call out intergroup conflicts and resolve them through open discussion.

I had a client who supervised a group of about a dozen people. She had a cold approach to her team, and she felt strongly that she didn't think it was appropriate to share vulnerabilities in the workplace. When I challenged her on this assumption, she thought about it and said that if she knew about her team's personal and professional challenges then she'd feel obligated to help them. She didn't want to get involved, so she protected herself from caring about them by not allowing any vulnerabilities at all.

When I shared with her the results of the studies around psychological safety, she was intrigued but skeptical. We discovered that her barrier to creating psychological safety was her assumption that she would then be responsible for fixing their problems. "Is that true?", I asked her. She sat back, considered the question and replied, "Maybe not."

Most of us resist vulnerability in professional settings because we may think that we have to somehow fix, solve, rescue or advise someone. What if we didn't? What if we empowered each other to solve our own problems? This opens up all sorts of possibilities, and as it turns out, vastly improves our performance as a team. So it may seem like a touchy feely concept dreamt up by social workers or bleeding heart hippies, but it actually came from a Harvard PhD candidate and has unlocked the secrets to humans working together in a more powerful way. It's the secret to how a tribe and its members can be most effective.

What Are You Tolerating?

This is my favorite question when I have a client who is feeling unappreciated, resentful or unfulfilled. We tolerate all sorts of things, and it can be useful to check in with ourselves. What we tolerate determines how our energy levels wax and wane. When we tolerate bad behavior, our energy levels dip. When we can reduce the things that drain us of energy, then we feel lighter.

This is an important question when we consider our tribe. If we are close to a person who is a net negative on our energy levels, then we are tolerating something in our lives that we know weighs us down. There are lots of reasons we might tolerate this, maybe this person is a relative or someone who helped you out when you needed it. Perhaps this person may really need support and you feel like you are the only one left for them.

The "average of five" exercise is a great way to determine what you are tolerating. If you have a few negatives, it might be important to understand the reason. How does it serve you to be connected to this person? How does this relationship impact you? How can you be amazing if you are close to a person who drains you of energy?

I have a client, Andy, who owns a personal training business. He works individually with clients and many of them become part of his tribe. Andy was struggling with one of his clients, Bob, because he didn't do the work, came each week full of complaints and had a very strong victim mentality. My client had provided a safe space for Bob to air his dirty laundry, but then felt obligated to help Bob solve his issues. Each week Bob would return with the same complaints, never taking Andy's advice. My client started to dread working with Bob and considered terminating him as a customer. Bob was draining him of energy and it was having a significant negative impact on him.

We challenged Andy's assumption that he needed to fix Bob's problems. We played with the idea that he could care about Bob without giving him advice or solutions. My client was great at creating psychological safety, but then he didn't know how to manage the rest of the process. When he created a strategy for how to serve his customers without having to fix them, he became a much more effective trainer and his tribe evolved into a source of energy gain rather than energy drain.

As a parent of two teenagers, I have taken this concept into our home. We share our vulnerabilities with each other often. We admit when we don't know something. We feel safe to tell each other when we've goofed. In fact, it's so engrained that it saved our daughter's life. Really. At the tender age of 12, she began feeling out of control emotionally. She was having scary thoughts and was overcome by the intensity and frequency of negative emotions. In order to cope with the emotional discomfort, she started to self-harm. She told me immediately after she did it, and there was no shame placed on her by us. After all, it was obvious that she was already ashamed without us piling on, hence, magnifying her issues. Each time she would hurt herself, she would come to us. When things got worse and she became suicidal, she came to us again. I can't imagine where we'd be if she didn't feel safe to tell us what was going on inside her head. I can't think about how much worse she'd be today if we had shamed her or reacted in a negative way. I can't wonder how else she may have handled her pain if she was all alone without a tribe to catch her, give her a hand and surround her with unconditional love. Because she could tell us the thing that she was thinking, she is alive today.

Judgment-Free Zone

I suffer from something I call FOWOT. It stands for Fear Of What Others Think. I find myself struggling to do things for fear of how I'll be judged. Many of my clients suffer from this too. One client doesn't want to seem like a patriarch. Another doesn't want to look like she doesn't know what she's doing. A third, worries that people won't approve of her new career choice. We depend on others for acceptance, approval and belonging. It's human. It's also something that can hold us back.

When we set out to create a tribe, one of the agreements we can make with each other is to do our best to release the urge to judge each other. I was part of a leadership team where we agreed from the very beginning that we would not speak negatively about anyone on the team if they were not present. I have to be honest that it was really hard to stick to the agreement. There were times when I felt justified in my smug indignation with a member of the team. However, it was far more effective for me to address the issue directly with the person than to say something negative about them to someone else.

When we set up agreements, we pay attention to how they are mutually beneficial. After all, why would I agree to do something if I didn't receive a benefit? For example, I ask my clients to agree to hide nothing and hold nothing back. The benefit is that they will be more powerfully served if they give me all the raw information without sugarcoating it or hiding some of the details. The benefit to me is that I can put together the puzzle. Likewise, boundaries are imaginary lines in the sand that we will not cross. They may be spoken or unspoken, but boundaries are created for me by me. They have nothing to do with other people. Instead, boundaries are like back up plans that I will follow if I get too close to a situation that makes me uncomfortable. If my father brings up politics which is a boundary that I will not cross with him because it typically doesn't go well, then I have an internal flag that pops up and reminds me to steer clear and change course. We both benefit because our relationship is protected. Both boundaries and agreements pave the way for people to connect openly and honestly with each other which then can build an awesome tribe.

When I create a group coaching program, I begin each session by asking everyone to leave their judgment at the door. In this way, everyone can feel safe to be vulnerable. Additionally, when you make a choice to not be judgmental, you'll find yourself being more open and curious. Judging others less allows for more empathy and compassion. When you can stop trying to make snap opinions about what another person is saying or doing, you slow your brain down and actually listen fully. It allows us to connect more deeply, which is part of the need that a tight tribe can satisfy.

Thinking Out Loud

I live by the mantra of, "How do you know what you think until you've said it out loud?" Not everyone is a verbal thinker, but we can all learn more about ourselves by reflecting and answering challenging questions with another person. This is another benefit of the tribe. They can hold a safe space for you to explore. They can walk with you as you work your way through life's difficulties. Speaking out loud the things that are going on in your mind and body are very effective ways to make progress.

John Stepper, author of *Working Out Loud,* makes the case that we can follow our passions without having to quit our day jobs. He started Working Out Loud circles, where people within any organization can come together to support each other in passionate projects. By creating a tribe of likeminded people, each person is in the circle to support and empower each other go after their life's dreams. Speaking about the dreams helps these tribe members achieve them.

I believe the biggest reason that coaching is such a transformational skillset is that is encourages a person to reflect and think out loud. I had a client whose supervisor was withholding information that was critical for her to do her job. She had asked her HR department for a transfer and was told it would take a few months. She was dreading having to work with her supervisor for one more day let alone a few more months and had a lot of resentment towards him. We worked on lowering the intensity of the negative emotions she held towards him, which she did by thinking out loud. Then we worked through a strategy that had her feeling hopeful rather than dreadful about the next two months. The key insight came when I asked her what stops her from intentionally spending more time with her supervisor to get to know him better. She responded that her ego was telling her that she was weak. She had unconsciously enrolled herself in a tug of war with her supervisor, and her ego was telling her not to let go of the rope. Once she had said it out loud, her ego quieted down and she was able to move forward. The discipline of having to reflect on yourself is that you have to put the puzzle together in a way that makes sense. Usually this exercise concludes with an insight that suddenly releases you from the very behavior you were trying to stop.

Finding a tribe of people with whom you can think out loud is key to self-development and growth. It's also a great way to solve problems that have plagued you for a long time. Having people in your life who can ask great questions that have you reflecting and making discoveries can get you unstuck. There are times when you will say something out loud that surprises and delights you. If you want to grow and continue to become better versions of yourself, then your tribe is everything.

SELF REFLECTIONS

1. How does your tribe build you up, empower you and energize you?

2. What are you tolerating that, if stopped, would provide relief and freedom in your life?

3. How many people do you have in your life who give you a safe space to think out loud, challenge your thoughts and have you best intentions at heart?

CHAPTER TWO.
NO BRAKES, ALL ACCELERATOR

*"Slow down and everything you are chasing
will come around and catch you."*

JOHN DE PAOLA

I love to hang out in idea land. It's a wonderful place with no limits. I float from idea to idea, accelerating from reality to places of unlimited possibility where things like mindsets and budgets and rules don't apply. As one idea comes up, it is followed by more ideas with more frequency and at a quicker pace. Picture me on a race track where around and around I go generating ideas on top of ideas, accelerating with each lap, but not actually going anywhere. Ask me to bring an idea to fruition and my tires blow out.

Possibility-gasm™

I'm sitting in a meeting with several community leaders, and a young professional's organization is presenting several new ideas they have for both growing their group and attracting young professionals to our city. Each new idea energizes me and I nod my head with excitement. That's a great idea, I think to myself. Huh. So is *that* idea. Oooh, I love that concept. And that one too. Give me more. Yes, yes...Yes!

This is what I call the possibility-gasm™. New ideas spark the possibility circuit in the brain, and suddenly I am running off into a utopian future with unicorns and world peace. If you are like me, your head is always swimming with new ideas. "It doesn't have to be that way" is how it all starts. If not this way, then what way? Each new idea associated with a current problem brings about the possibility of solving it. Because it feels amazing to be in the possibility-gasm™, new ideas are intensely attractive.

There is a spectrum, right? All brakes means saying no to everything, while all accelerator means saying yes to everything. Both extremes can be troublesome. For people who think differently, we gravitate towards the all accelerator side. It can backfire by saddling you with no time, no focus, and no impact. Think gerbil wheel.

For example, I really struggled with saying yes to all the ideas that came my way. I could always see the benefits and rarely cared about the risks. When my two children were still in diapers and I was working full-time, I chose to get an MBA in night school. An MBA was an idea that was bursting with opportunities for me to climb the corporate ladder, launch a new business or some other world dominating theme. I also chose to be the sole caretaker for my ill grandmother, because the idea of nurturing and caring for her filled my heart with love, connection and honor. Lastly, I said yes to projects at work that included traveling, since I would learn so much, gain valuable expertise and build up my resume.

Unsurprisingly, I retained very little in MBA School. I resented my family for not helping me with my grandma. I resented my husband for not helping more with the kids. I was not present for anyone. I was exhausted, stressed and eventually developed walking pneumonia. In short, I fell on my face.

Perhaps a natural course correction would be to say no. To everything. I have a client who chose this approach. When he came to see me, he couldn't take on any new ideas because he was waiting for his partner to join in with him. He passed up all sorts of opportunities saying that he needed his partner to be ready too. He was full of resentment; frustrated and insecure. By saying no to everything, his fears seemed to expand in both frequency and intensity. Not only did he blame his partner for not wanting to take on new adventures, but he was unsure if he even knew where to start if he embarked on them alone.

The common theme for both approaches is that all yes and all no can end in misery. A good way to move towards the middle of the spectrum is to make an agreement with yourself not to commit to an answer impulsively. By then, the effects of the possibility-gasm™ will have worn off.

Is It Ego or Authentic Self?

A powerful distinction that can be made is which self is energized by new ideas. There is the ego, which is looking for power, control and status. The ego loves to think of how people will perceive us if a new idea can be carried out. For example, I have a client who wants to write a book. When I asked how being a published author would impact her life, she responded with the fact that she can tell people she is a published author. That sounds like the ego talking. "I'll take some status with a side of bragging rights, please."

I have another client who was stuck in an industry where he felt he couldn't escape. Each idea he threw on the table was met with intense excitement. When we would dig a little further, he seemed to be dependent upon how others would see him if he succeeded with the idea, like his Board would start taking him seriously, he could break into a different industry or he could build up his status and reputation in the community. Every idea had him at the center. As a result, he was never able to implement his ideas. The catch with the ego is that it hates challenge and change. The ego wants him safe, which means thinking, behaving and feeling the same. New ideas may be alluring to the ego, but it'll be hard to keep up the required momentum and bring them to fruition.

The authentic self is also energized by new ideas, but it's from an impact mindset. The possibility of ending suffering in some form for others is the goal. The authentic self gets fired up about how new ideas can serve others, not ourselves. If my client wanted to write a book because she wants to open up the dialogue around a difficult subject, offer hope to those who have lost it and empower people to make better choices, then that sounds more like it's coming from the authentic self. Coming from one's authentic place requires some bravery, to not be afraid of ourselves. We're used to living in our own little nests that feel safe to us.

One of my clients decided she wanted to create a culture steeped in personal growth and development. She wanted her entire team to feel empowered and become better versions of themselves. Her focus was squarely set on her team, not herself, and she was able to stay motivated and inspired. Each hurdle was met with a drive to get around it so she could get back to the business of making her team better. The results are that the business doubled in less than a year. The team had taken on more leadership roles within the organization, freeing her up to do the high-level work and take an unplugged vacation (her first ever). Her favorite story is of the team wallflower who volunteered to take on a leadership role to train her group on a new software package, which amazed her coworkers and supervisor.

When I can distinguish between which self is excited about a new idea, it helps me to say no. When I allow my authentic self to lead the way, I find that I am more in alignment and have sustainable energy. For many of us who don't think like everyone else in the room, we can easily burn out by following ALL the ideas. Additionally, too many ideas can lead to poor follow through. I can honestly say that I have the best intentions when I agree to something, but I've lost count of the times that I haven't followed through. Either I forget, run out of time or lose motivation. Then I beat myself up for not being able to finish what I've started. Now, I only take on projects that excite my authentic self and let the rest go.

Let me also share that my authentic self gets enthusiastic about a lot of ideas too, so distinguishing which self is charged up isn't always enough. There are loads of problems in the world and multiple solutions to each one. When a new idea gets thrown on the table, I can get lost in the possibility-gasm™. In the afterglow, my energy falls when I realize the difficulties of actually carrying out the idea, and I feel drained. The details of the idea feel like a wet blanket on a roaring fire.

Looking at Life from 30,000 ft.

My different thinking tends to be at the 30,000 foot level. I love it up here because I don't have to actually figure out how to achieve the goal. Instead, I can stay in my high energy zone of possibility and imagine a world where middle school doesn't have to suck, where large corporations care more for their people than their bottom line and where we can have discussions about difficult subjects without our judgments getting in the way. It's friggin awesome up here.

This is where visionaries live. It is easier not to deal with the details. Details prevent creativity and brainstorming. Don't kill my buzz, dude.

However, an idea that never gets implemented is just a dream. If I can't get an idea to the strategy phase, then it cannot help others, be of service, or have impact. Great ideas shouldn't have to tolerate being put on the shelf.

When we are all energized during a good brainstorming session, we may be imagining what it'd look like to carry out these ideas. Dopamine is a brain chemical that is released as a result of anticipating something good to come, like the possibility that accompanies an idea. If you are brainstorming with others, then some oxytocin may get released as a result of bonding with each other. This is all to say that the high is real and delicious. The catch is we mustn't overlook coming back down to earth and getting to work.

Balancing Yourself

Because I am on an unending quest to know myself better, I sought out an Enneagram consultant who came highly recommended by several colleagues. He sent me a questionnaire with one of the questions being what job would be a total nightmare for me? The answer is obvious: project manager; laying out a plan, filling in all the details, sequencing them so they happen in the proper order, prioritizing items. YUCK! This exercise highlighted my need to have a detail person on my team. A yin to my yang; someone on the ground so I can stay soaring at 30,000 feet. If you've worked with coaches or self-development junkies, then you already know we love to use assessments. For me to find a complementary teammate, there are several that can be used, like Kolbe, Meyers-Briggs, StrengthsFinder and Enneagram. While I won't put *all* my faith in any single assessment, I plan to use them as confirmation for what I think I already know.

By pairing myself with a details person, I can exercise my greatest strength, which is to think differently than everyone else in the room. Being a visionary is a great thing. I no longer have to beat myself up for not being good at scheduling, prioritizing or planning. Instead, I can surround myself with people who can help in the areas where I am not robust so we are all working in our areas of strength. It's seems to me like a better use of my energy to get better at the things I am already naturally good at rather than try to shore up weaknesses.

As I surround myself with people whose strengths balance out my "weaknesses", I find that I am so much more efficient. I can cruise between 30,000 feet and sea level easily. I can check myself with people who are not different thinkers to make sure I'm not missing something. I can request feedback from the people around me to make sure I am behaving well. Asking for help from people who enjoy the kinds of things I don't is a win-win.

I used to be concerned about asking for help, because I assumed if someone agreed to help me that they secretly didn't want to and would later resent me. Talk about projection! I have spent so much of my life resenting others for not reading my mind. Go figure. I used to say yes because I wanted people to like me, only to get in over my head doing work I didn't like and resent *them* for all of it. It's as though I had no other choice than to say yes. Once I started saying no to things I didn't want to do, the resentment mysteriously vanished. (Insert smirk here.) Once the resentment disappeared, it was much easier to ask for help and remain unattached to the answer.

Alignment

One of the main benefits of learning and accepting who I am is to align myself. I like to think of Aesop's fable about a man and his son bringing their donkey to the town market. The man is walking to town with his son and donkey, and a passerby laughs at him and asks why he would force his son to walk when he has a perfectly good donkey to carry him. So the man puts his son on the donkey and they continue their trek to town.

Another passerby laughs at him and says how rude of the son to let his father walk when the boy is young and strong. So the man puts his son on the ground and climbs on the donkey himself. And off they go to town.

A third passerby laughs at him and says how cruel of you to ride while your son trudges along. So the man lifts up his son and they both ride the donkey.

As they approach town, some people cluck at him saying how unkind he is to put so much weight on the poor donkey. So the man and the son get off the donkey, grab a pole and tie the donkey's feet to it so they can carry the donkey into town. As they are crossing the bridge, the donkey kicks a foot loose causing the boy to drop his end and the donkey falls off the bridge and drowns in the river below. The moral of the story: Please all, and you will please none.

One decision that I struggle with every three years is whether or not to run for my elected position on our local School Board. I began 7 years ago as an angry parent, but quickly experienced the amazing impact I could have on our students, employees and community. I was hooked after my first year. However, it is a big-time strain and I am not compensated well, financially or otherwise. In fact, I've been sworn at, protested against and even had to walk through an angry mob once. As my term is coming up at the end of this year, I am pondering how this aligns with who I assume I am and who I *really* am in the world. I have a vested interest in our district, because I have two children who attend it. It's fulfilling to have a positive impact and improve the lives of others. On the other hand, there are others who can serve and it takes up so much of my time, which is hard on my family, my business and myself. As you can see, alignment is not always obvious and I will have to use my head, heart and gut as I move towards a final decision. I will keep in mind that if I aim to please all, then I please none.

Serving Over Pleasing

The fable reminds me that pleasing others isn't valuable. The name of the game is serving others. With this in mind, I need to be absolutely clear on what ideas will serve others AND align with who I am. Sure, I want to save puppies, end war, eliminate child abuse and ensure every adult is literate. By checking in with my authentic self, I can make a wise choice. Because, believe me, I will take on all the causes of the world to live in the possibility-gasm™ but then never actually accomplish anything. By tapping the brakes, I can go farther with more energy in my reserve tank.

When I began coaching, I was really good at pleasing my clients. I wanted them to like me, believing trust would come from them being fond of me as a person. When I found a master coach to work with me, I quickly discovered that this coach was serving me powerfully and couldn't give one darn whether or not I liked him. He would say things that made me cringe. He would interrupt me in the middle of my sentences. He would challenge my assumptions. He'd ask me direct questions then corral me as I tried to avoid giving a straight answer. While I didn't always like him, I respected the heck out of him. I have experienced more growth with this coach than anyone else in my life. By serving me, he was helping me become my most powerful self. He could "see" who I am and he called it out of me, even if it risked me getting mad, swearing at him, or speaking unkindly about him behind his back.

As I started to dive into the world of serving over pleasing, I am still surprised how hard it is to do. How can I tell my client it's obvious he isn't paying attention and ask him to do so? How can I tell a client that her biggest block is from her need to judge others in order to feel better about herself? How can I interrupt a client and redirect her to answer the question instead of avoiding, over-explaining, or justifying? When I do these things, I am incredibly uncomfortable but I know that my purpose is to serve others not indulge or appease them. It helps that I make an agreement with my clients to that affect so they aren't caught off guard, but it's still tough.

When I serve instead of please, my clients actually thank me. While they may not like to be questioned, challenged, or given feedback, they feel understood and seen. Many remark they actually feel relieved when I call them out. They say that they needed someone to shine a light on their blind spot, because they didn't know what it was. They say that my compassionate truth telling shifted their perspective and their entire world changed as a consequence. They say that while it can feel like a slap in the face, it forced them to see something that caused a breakthrough. With these results, not being liked seems like a small price to pay.

SELF REFLECTIONS

1. If you are great at generating ideas but lack follow through, then how can you deliberately slow yourself down?

2. Who do you know who can help you increase the likelihood that your ideas come true?

3. What can you do to shift from being a people pleaser to a person who serves others powerfully?

CHAPTER THREE.
THINKING DIFFERENTLY IS AN ASSET

"Here's to the crazy ones — the misfits, the rebels, the troublemakers, the round pegs in the square holes. The ones who see things differently — they're not fond of rules. You can quote them, disagree with them, glorify or vilify them, but the only thing you can't do is ignore them because they change things."

STEVE JOBS

learned at a young age that I had to think like everyone else if I wanted to fit in. There was safety in the herd. Even though I didn't always agree with people, I didn't share my thoughts for fear of being caste out or thrown off the island. I assumed my different thinking was a liability that I needed to hide. I was able to hide it for about 30 years, so I really believed in my assumption. I now know that my different thinking is a gift and asset. When I started using it, I had impact, I changed people's lives, and I became unstoppable. This thing that I lugged around in secret was actually my greatest strength.

29

Speak Up

Because I could hide my different thinking, I was able to survive high school being a member of the popular group. I was a social chameleon who could fit in anywhere with almost anyone. It was a huge source of pride for me. I got asked to all the dances. I was invited to parties on the weekends. I spent very little time at home because my social calendar was always full. To be clear, I never shared how I thought with my peers. I told myself that I was wrongheaded and just go along with the group. I denied my own values and integrity. The internal conflict was intense and constant.

My hiding carried over into my schoolwork and eventually my career. In classes where there was more than one answer, I really struggled. I typically did not come to the same conclusions as my classmates in subjects like English and Social Studies. My teachers mostly reinforced my beliefs that my different thinking was not valued, so I felt validated in keeping my thoughts to myself. I experienced an epiphany in Math and Science though. In these subjects, I could get the same answer as everyone else. At the time, this gave me a roadmap for my future. Go into engineering young woman, for you will find your place amongst your people.

Off to my engineering gig I went each day, and I would return home exhausted, frustrated, and confused. Nothing felt very fulfilling, and I was constantly wondering why the systems and processes were set up in a way that didn't treat people very well. Interestingly, I cared very little about the technical problems and found myself naturally drawn to people problems. Dare I speak up and advocate for something better? Dare I expose my thoughts for improvement? Dare I buck the system and risk being noticed as an outsider? Until a few years ago, the answer was always a resounding no.

My first job out of college was working in the oil field. After my 6 months of training in the field, I was placed in Louisiana. As a female, engineer from Chicago, I didn't exactly fit in. I was in the field with the operators, and they had no interest in having to deal with a Yankee, women engineer. I made it my personal goal to win them over. They played all sorts of tricks on me, like driving really fast so they lost me on the way to our work sites or putting pebbles in my hubcaps so that everyone would laugh when I drove up. I took all in good jest and chalked it up to harmless hazing. It never occurred to me that I was tolerating bad behavior. I never considered that I was being humiliated for their pleasure. I never spoke up. I just kept showing up and fighting to fit in, which I did eventually. Of course, I had to change who I was to do it, but, hey, if fitting in was the goal then I achieved it.

At the same time, I greatly admired people who would speak up. I wished I could be more like them. One of the things that my children have done for me is to challenge my fears. When they started school, I got involved and did my regular fitting in routine. I didn't make waves, just played my "win them over" act. When our son was in 2nd grade, we witnessed some terrible behaviors from his teacher. Even thought I had spent my entire life never speaking up for myself, I was able to do it for our son. Most parents and other teachers said they didn't feel like the behavior was all that bad, but I didn't care and certainly didn't agree with what they thought. I found the courage to bring it to her attention, and then the attention of the principal. In short, I made a big stink. Some people distanced themselves from me as a result. Some teachers stopped talking with me. The principal placated me, but he also let this teacher's behavior continue. It was a painful time for our family. Here's the thing. Every once in a while, another parent would pull me aside and thank me for saying something. They felt as I did but didn't know how to handle it. Because I shared my thoughts on how things could be better, other people benefitted. And <u>there</u> is the power. Because I don't see the world the way most people do, I can offer a different perspective that can result in better and more innovative solutions.

Because I was highly dissatisfied with the way our public education system was operating, I decided to run for school board. This forced me to throw my different thinking out into the community and allow people to judge me publicly. There is an inflection point that occurs when you decide to stop complaining and do something. If you don't like something, then get a seat at the table, take action and be significant. I ran for election. I participated in debates. I was interviewed by local newspapers, the morning radio show, and businesses. It was the first time in my life that I was acknowledged and rewarded for my different thinking. I won the election and received the most votes, even more than the incumbent. This was a new epiphany. Perhaps my different thinking wasn't such a liability after all.

Unlock Potential

A great way to shift how we think is to challenge each other. When I say challenge, I don't mean fight or argue or debate. I mean getting curious about something and ask questions in an effort to understand better. If we are all thinking the same way, then we may not have opportunities to have our thinking challenged. What I now know is that challenging underlying beliefs and assumptions shifts mindsets and unlocks potential.

When I ask my clients a really powerful question, my favorite response is silence. When they have to stop their urge to provide an answer without thoughtful reflection, I know I have engaged their higher level thinking. You can almost see the shift in their perception occurring real-time, like two tectonic plates slowly moving into a new position. As a result, my clients will come back and share with me how different the world seems to them since their discovery. They report feeling lighter and empowered and confident and hopeful and excited. I think that's what unlocking potential feels like.

I had two powerful conversations with a potential client named Bob, a 45 year old who owned his own small business and had two young children. He described to me how exhausted and frantic he felt. He had loads of internal conflict, and the voices in his head were constantly chirping at him to be better, help everyone, and never let 'em see you sweat. A visual of a one-armed paper hanger comes to mind. After just one conversation, he had a total shift in his thinking. Bob realized he had created a box for himself. We addressed his fears of leaving the box, and agreed to talk again in a few weeks. When we met, Bob reported feeling totally different. He said his personal and professional relationships all improved as a result of the shift in his mindset. He also permitted himself to challenge the voices that had him hustling all the time. He slowed down. He listened to his body. He unlocked a potential that he hadn't been actively seeking, which was to deepen his connections with the people he loved.

By moving someone's mindset just a small amount, they can see the world differently. We all have psychological barriers that hold us back. The beauty of not thinking like everyone else in the room is that offering a new idea can motivate others to challenge how they think about things. We know that challenging our own thoughts leads to a higher evolution of thinking. If we can all evolve our own thinking and facilitate it for our fellow humans, we can all stand to find more peace, joy, and purpose in our lives.

Inspire the Challenge

I worked in and with big corporations for 20 years. I hid my different thinking so I could fit in, but deep inside I knew that I didn't agree with most of the corporate practices, behaviors, and policies that I witnessed. When I was elected to the school board, I again found myself wondering what the heck was going on around here. I didn't see a concerted effort to challenge the status quo. There was resistance to change the system. The board itself was dysfunctional, and we were unable to work well together. Over the course of 7 years, I shared what I thought was possible. I exposed my different thinking. When everyone was looking left, I asked them to look right. Over 7 years, our board and school district have witnessed big changes for the better. In our quest to challenge the status quo, we inspired unlikely candidates to run for the board and become part of our band of misfits. I've learned that the cost of being chastised and unloved is worth it, because other people will pop up and join your cause.

I have a client who is currently working in a large corporation. He is unfulfilled and fatigued most of the time. He thinks his company treats its employees poorly, and he is constantly standing up for his team and protecting them from the system. During one of our sessions, he shared that he would love to leave his corporate job but worried about who would stand up for his people in his stead. I asked him if he thought they could stand up for themselves because he had inspired them to do so. He responded with multiple stories of how previous members of his teams had moved on and became advocates for themselves. He actually sat up taller and prouder as he thought about how he had inspired others to say no to unacceptable requests and create boundaries for themselves.

When we witness a person speaking for what they believe, it's hard to deny that it is a captivating experience. As I watch some of my clients, who are mostly people like me, I am in awe of how they command attention and action when they speak about how they see things. It does motivate me to do the same, especially when I am afraid of what others will think of me and perhaps decide they don't like me *or* my ideas. My possibility-gasm gets all revved up at the thought of a world where people are free and safe to share what they think.

What Are They Really Saying

When I decided to stop hiding the way I think, something really interesting happened. I discovered that my curiosity was able to come out and play. The first thing that happened was my relationships started to improve. The ones that were already good became more intimate. The ones that weren't so good became easier and less stressful. The ones that were toxic, I terminated. I was able to get away from exploring how I was somehow contributing to others' behaviors and instead, I observed them just behaving. I no longer took things personally. I recognized and embraced letting go of their reactions. I honored them by allowing them to behave however they liked without the need to judge them for it. It felt liberating and blissful.

Meet Ann, a 28-year-old client, who is an entrepreneur and small business owner. She struggles with her stepparent. It's the typical Cinderella story where the stepparent is threatened by the stepchild and excludes her from the inner circle of the family. She described in great detail how her stepparent repeatedly denied Ann from belonging to her family. My client was always kept on the outside and was allowed in only when the stepparent okayed it. It was, and still is, a painful experience for Ann. When she spends time with the family, she has to be vigilant to protect herself so she doesn't get hurt. Obviously, she just wants to be herself and quit the exhausting game of putting up walls when she's with them.

We decided to pick apart one example of a hurtful thing the stepparent had done. When Ann shared the harsh statement her stepparent had said to her, I asked Ann what she thought the stepparent was really trying to say. Ann got quiet. She stared at me, almost in disbelief. She replied that her stepparent obviously hated her. I got more curious. What was going on with the stepparent that she was saying a hurtful thing? Can we dig under the surface and find the nugget of truth? What if the comment had nothing to do with my client? I knew I had engaged a higher level of thinking when Ann said nothing.

By asking Ann to step back and look at it from the outside, she was able to give me an answer. It turned out that the stepparent saw Ann as a threat to the financial stability of the family. If you think you are running out of money, then you lash out at anyone who may want to put their hands in the coffers. Instead of seeing this as an attack on Ann, it was an attack based on a fear, like a dog barking at the mailman. The mailman doesn't take the dog barking personally and wonders if he is a bad person. Instead, he recognizes that the dog is feeling threatened and he simply walks away. Ann's assumption about the stepparent's comment shifted. She didn't suddenly feel all lovey dovey for her stepparent, but she was able to find a way to better understand where the comment originated, which had very little to do with Ann. By trying to understand why a person might act a certain way, she was able to decouple her own worthiness from any comments her stepparent might make.

Imagine being able to allow other people to say and do things and not have it mean anything about you. Possibility-gasm™! If you don't think like everyone else, then you can focus on different things too. When you can ponder different possibilities for the true purpose of behaviors and actions, you can extract yourself from the crazy-making that happens sometimes when humans say mean things to each other.

Learning and Growth

We have all experienced growth and learning as a result of overcoming a fear or obstacle. If you are not like everybody else, then there have probably been times in your life where you felt like you didn't belong or were on the outside. Being different can be daunting and difficult.

Out of difficulties grow miracles.

JEAN DE LA BRUYERE

I'm not sure about the miracles part, but I do know that I have had the most intense learning when I am in struggle. I wish it weren't so, but I learned not to touch the hot stove by experiencing the burn of touching a hot stove. I chalk it up to human nature. We need to do, experience and try things for ourselves. If I want to learn and grow, then I'd better get comfortable with discomfort.

For me, my different thinking caused me discomfort which is why I avoided and hid it. I didn't see the payoff of being uncomfortable. What I've learned is that I had to face my fears, take risks, and make mistakes to become a better version of myself. I had to do the thing that I had spent my life running from: risk not fitting in. When I did it, it felt yucky, scary and edgy. When I did it repeatedly, the bad feelings became less intense and I found other likeminded individuals who supported me. It was such a glorious discovery that I soon looked forward to the discomfort that led to growth. No, I'm not a sadist who enjoys being uncomfortable, but I have stopped running from the discomfort and allowed it to wash over me like a cold shower in the winter time. Yes, it feels terrible and awful, yet I do it because I know that there is something delightful on the other side. Just like when your parent released their grip from the bicycle that first time, there was a moment of sheer terror immediately followed by a sense of exhilaration as you peddled your way down the sidewalk by yourself.

Middle school has not been good to our family. Both of our children experienced some incredibly painful experiences there. Our daughter, who is compassionate, kind and gentle, was being eaten alive by her peers. She tried to fit in but never could find solid footing. She was repeatedly kicked out of groups, which happens to everyone, but she took it really hard. She would go into a deep hole and found it nearly impossible to get out of it. In the 8th grade, our daughter was once again excommunicated from a group of girls. Don't even get me started on the role social media has played in magnifying these experiences. She began to implode. We tried to reason with her, give her coping strategies and had her makes plans for how to get through it. Alas, one day, after a particularly terrible day, she looked at me and asked why she had to keep going back to that mean building. Talk about different thinking! It was a powerful question that shifted our mindset.

We came to the realization that she didn't have to go back there. With all the possibilities for education in the 21st century, she had choices that may suit her better. She chose online schooling, and she changed overnight. No more dread. No more anxiety. No more trying to fit in. Instant relief. For her. For me, I crashed into the deep, dark hole. I couldn't sleep. I lost my appetite. I felt like a failure as a parent. I was filled with worry. Were we running away? What if she never learned to make friends? How come other kids could do it and not her? While this was happening, I reminded myself that I needed to stay in the discomfort and not run from it. I liken it to forcing myself to sit in my own dirty diaper and refusing to change it. It is unbelievably uncomfortable. But I knew that I would probably learn something and gain some insight if I didn't deny the discomfort.

What I learned is that my daughter is an incredible young lady. She advocated for her needs, and we listened. She started online schooling, and she is doing well. By listening to her, she felt safe to share her solutions with us and learned that we have her back. Our relationship also improved, an unspoken trust showed up to let us know we are in this together. We challenge each other's thinking, and then we proceed with what feels like the right option. And if it doesn't work, then we repeat the process. Not only are we modeling our intention to continuously learn and grow, we are showing our children that discomfort isn't the enemy. It's a part of life, and we can support each other when we are in it. Our children have entered the world knowing that their different thinking should never be hidden or seen as a liability. Instead, it is an asset that brings both discomfort and growth.

SELF REFLECTIONS

1. How has your out-of-the-box thinking been an asset to you and others?

2. How can you surround yourself with people who challenge your thinking?

3. What would you do if other's rejection of your ideas has nothing to do with you?

CHAPTER FOUR.
I AM THE BOTTLENECK

"A man stands in his own shadow and wonders why it's dark."

ZEN PROVERB

A s an engineer who designed oil refineries for nearly 20 years, I think "bottleneck" is a great term to describe the one variable, if it were changed, would speed up the entire process. This makes sense if it's a pump or a heat exchanger or even the rate of a chemical reaction, but it can also be true for human processes. Many of the entrepreneurs, visionaries and small business owners who are my clients are burning the candle at both ends. They are simultaneously the person who is driving the pace of growth and throttling it.

Bright Shiny Object Syndrome

So if you are an idea factory, like me, then you know how easy it is to be distracted. New ideas, theories, books, podcasts and TED talks represent bright, shiny objects that demand our attention. I can be knee deep in proposals, chapter deadlines, and networking follow-ups and find myself saying yes to a great initiative that shows up in my email. Possibility-gasm™! What if I could make such and such happen? What if we could change this and that forever? What if I could bring so and so into this? Sign me up!

I had a client who was an extraordinary visionary. She swam in the worlds of philosophy and organizational development. She ran a small business in the financial industry, and she sought my help with growing the business with intention and purpose. She was a dream client for a coach because I only had to prompt her with powerful questions and then sit back and watch the magic. She would connect the dots, make discoveries and create a strategy all in the course of an hour-long session.

Shortly after working together, she asked me to join her in leading her team in a developmental conversation about growing the business. It was in this meeting that I witnessed her Achilles heel. She was so in tune with everyone on her team that she was like a master conductor directing all of them in their own solo performances. Together they created beautiful music, but they couldn't do it without her being present. She had effectively painted herself into a corner.

It turned out the biggest bottleneck to growth was herself. The things that had made her such a successful and high achieving business owner were precisely the things that were holding her back from growing the business. I got the sense that the team knew it too. They made comments during the meeting about how they would be able to handle the workflow. They questioned her about how they could answer their own questions, make their own judgment calls and have some more authority for decisions. As she described the new structure for the business, the team members wondered if this was another shiny, new object. Would she follow through? Would she be able to let go of control? Would she get distracted by another theory, principle or idea for growing the business?

Without knowing it she became a hindrance to her team rather than a nourishing conduit for them to succeed without having to rely on her holding their hands. She needed to trust her team, the very "child" she created and cultivated into a well-oiled functioning machine...like a Super Bowl caliber coach watching her team from the sidelines with total confidence, they can succeed without her running onto the field after each play, thereby, minimizing their own ability to achieve a touchdown on their own merit. It's like a well-intentioned parent who has trouble trusting the values they instilled in their child and allowing the child to realize their own potential on their own. Letting go of something you love is the most arduous lesson.

My client did choose to let go of control, and she did it in a slow and measured fashion. She didn't take any huge leaps, just small steps heading in the right direction. She tested the waters of responsibility and trust, and when things went well, she tested a little more. Bit by bit, her team showed her that they were ready for more leadership opportunities which improved how they thought of themselves and each other. My client's big ideas were easier for the team to tolerate, because they were all closer to operating in their own wheelhouses; my client in her 30,000 foot view, and the rest in their ground level stations. If she threw new ideas at them, they knew she would take care of the high-level vision stuff and wait for the strategic planning work to sift its way to them. Win win.

Burn Out

It is common for people who work with big idea types to get burned out by all the, "Hey, I got an idea" remarks. Pairing big picture people with detail-oriented people sounds like a no brainer. However, the detail folks get irritated with the big vision people and vice versa. I have a client who runs a small retail business. He is one of the biggest picture guys I've ever met. He has hired several detail-oriented types, which made sense to me when I started working with them.

At our first consult, he was difficult to corral as he loved dreaming up new innovations for his organization. In fact, each idea spurred 10 new ideas for him. As I watched the interactions between him and his team, I could see that they were burning out just being the same room with him. I envision the team thinking, "Oh, my gosh, he just added hours and hours to my already overflowing workload". He couldn't seem to get anyone excited enough to play idea-ball with him. Both sides seemed a bit frustrated, and consequently, we didn't make much progress that day.

As I continued to work with this group, it was clear that this client was exhausting his team. In addition, all decisions went through him, meaning the team members had to rely on him and his shiny, ball problem to give them the go ahead. Each time they asked for a decision, he would come up with several other ideas instead of just giving them a thumbs up or down. By advocating for their needs, the team members found a way to let my client know they were ready for more leadership. When they could have some control over their own destiny, the entire shop became more efficient and fluent.

Unload the Bottleneck

So what does one do if they are so inspired by all the amazing ideas out there that they cannot stay focused on the task at hand? If there is something about having my cake and eating it too, then I am all in. There is a way, and it involves being able to let go of some things. When I work with my clients around control, we let go of small things first and build up a level of confidence that the sky won't cave and the business won't go bankrupt. If you are the bottleneck, then it may be control is the thing that stands in your way.

I had a client who was the supervisor of a small team in a large, corporate company. She wanted to do a good job. She wanted to make a difference. She wanted to get promoted into the VP role. She had some huge ideas that would transform the business. Yet she spent most of her time wallowing in the minutia of the day to day work. She was unwilling to let go of things that could be done by others because she didn't believe deep down that they would do a good enough job. Well, unfortunately, you can't have it both ways. You can't do the high-level thinking and visioning if you also have to do the daily tasks and managing of people. She was caught in this quandary, and she wanted to find a way out.

The way out was for her to let go. She had to turn over decisions to others. She had to let people help her get her job done. She had to turn over authority to her team members. It wasn't easy. Sometimes she'd hand things over then take them back. Sometimes she'd manage people who didn't need managing. Sometimes she found mistakes that others made and felt justified in her need to control. But she persevered because she knew she was the bottleneck. By de-bottlenecking herself, she boosted her own work and was able to begin initiating some of her big and hefty ideas.

I had another client who worked in a large organization that didn't really fulfill her passion. Because this job helped her meet all her financial obligations, she asked if she could showcase her passion for event planning within the organization. When they would have a department meeting, she would come up with outrageous ideas and implement them. She was a wizard at whipping up creative foods, neat decorations, and unique gift concepts. She was absolutely energized when she was in the planning stages.

Then the event would come up, and she'd work herself to sheer exhaustion. She would carry out every single item on her wish list. Alone. During these weeks, she would show up for the coaching calls weak and apathetic. She would say that she'd be better when the event was over. She couldn't see that her passion for creating an amazing vision for an event was being crushed by trying to make it come to fruition all by herself. Because she feared that nobody else would care as much as she did, she carried on with the mindset of just surviving it rather than relishing it like when she was in the visioning process. It's the "I'll be better when it's over" syndrome.

When we explored what was keeping her from asking for help, it came back to control which is a coping mechanism for fear. She had this fairy tale vision that was absolutely perfect. She had to defend its perfection by not letting anyone lay a hand on it, like a mother bear protecting her cub. When she could imagine her vision being carried out with the help of others, she felt both relief *and* apprehension. By starting slowly, she overcame the apprehension part and subsequently the relief started to build. She came to discover that her visions could truly emerge even when other people had their hands on it. As she unloaded her plate, she found even more energy to create amazing visions. It was a positive reinforcement loop. The more she let go, the more she could create.

You Are Wearing Me Out

Most idea generators can identify the moment they have worn out their welcome. For many of us, it'll be with our spouses and children first. When I utter the words, "Hey guys, I have an idea", my family scatters like roaches when the lights come on. They have been subjected to my new idea phenomenon for years and years. With my possibility-gasm™ button triggered easily, they have watched many of my big ideas come and go. They know better than to get too excited or worried about any of my ideas, regardless of my eagerness when I propose them.

I am married to detail-oriented man. He loves details. He's a designer, and he flows when he gets into the details of highly complicated machinery. He makes lists for his lists in an ever-expanding cascade of lists. He plans everything down to the nth degree. So imagine what it's like for him when I approach him with yet another new idea to take the kids to Liberia for a 10 day leadership program. I see the endless promise of possibility, like the kids making connections with Liberians, learning how to empower others, experiencing the discomfort of being in a 3rd world, having their hearts touched by abject poverty, and on and on and on. My husband, on the other hand, thinks about the visas, vaccines, travel arrangements, transferring of funds to pay for it, kennel reservations for our pets, etc. I am high. He is not. Now imagine this scene occurring several days each week for over 19 years.

We have come to a place in our lives where I am free to propose ideas, as long as I consider them first and am able to answer the detail questions. My family is free to share their thoughts with me honestly and freely. I have committed to hearing their feedback and they are open to hearing mine. It's not a perfect system. To date, we are 50-50 on going to Liberia. It's girls against boys or big picture against detail oriented. We are still talking. And still together.

I have a client who is an out-of-the-box thinker. He always has a new idea or concept that he is game to try. He has a staff who is really good at making his dreams a reality. The problem occurs in that they cannot make every dream a reality. So all of his big, bold ideas are met with a deep sigh and immediate resistance. I have witnessed on several occasions this client trying to sell the idea to his staff, and his staff meeting him with unending "what if" scenarios. His energy is high. Their energy is low.

The more he tries to pump them up, the more they try to drag him back to earth. Both ends of the spectrum of possibility are reached so that the final product is <u>no</u> movement, a check-mate on both sides.

After working with me, when he wants to present a new idea to the group, he takes the time to think it through first. By the time he shares it with his staff, he's had a chance to think through which people will be most affected and who will have to do the most work. He weighs this against his own judgment for whether or not his people can handle the added responsibilities. Then, and only then, does he bring the idea to the team. He also asks for feedback and actually listens to what his team says, which means he uses their feedback as a compass. His team feels heard and he gets a sense of how this idea might move forward, by whom and at what pace. When he stopped burning out his dream fulfillers, his new ideas were met with much more consideration.

Here is a summary of 4 easy steps to increasing the likelihood of others accepting your ideas.

Step 1. Dream big. Go ahead and trigger the possibility-gasm™. Throw all the ideas on the table.

Step 2. Assess reality. Trade what you hope can happen with what is reality.

Step 3. Refine idea. Trim and pare the unrealistic parts of the idea.

Step 4. Promote idea. Deliberately choose to whom you will introduce your idea. Think strategic types.

Pick Your Battles

Because I never run out of ideas, I have been able to drain myself trying to start them up, get supports in place, manage the process and then scale it. In the beginning, I get all fired up to go into battle and find people to join me in my latest quest. Then, the motivation begins to wane. The details start to get in the way. Life happens. Things slow to a crawl and yet another idea fades into the sunset. This is the life cycle of most of my ideas before I became a coach.

If you meet me with a fresh idea, you will hear a woman that is prepared to go slay dragons to get it done. My passion around possibility knows no bounds, so watch out if I'm proposing a new idea. I have been known to advocate hard for something only to find myself wondering a few weeks later what the heck I was so enthusiastic about. All of this is to say it is helpful to know which battles to fight. If you are like me, then maybe you fight all of them, win a few and leave the battlefield defeated and really tired.

I am on the school board in my little Wisconsin community. We have about 800 teachers, and I have come to know the ones that are different thinkers. Kindred spirits. We had a teacher who was absolutely stellar with his kids. He connected with them so powerfully that they commonly came back well after graduating just to visit with him. He was a big idea guy, and he was constantly changing the way he did things in his classroom. I really respected him and loved to philosophize about how much better our education system would be if only...

Our state had gone through a painful process of decertifying teachers' unions. It pitted our community members against each other, and our teachers felt really unappreciated and unnecessarily targeted. This came after years of budget deficits and really difficult cuts to programs and staffing. This teacher had been advocating for years for all his innovative ideas. He had fought all the battles. He had won some and lost some. When the district instituted another cost saving measure, he had hit his upper limit. He chose to challenge the new policy, even though the policy itself wasn't a big deal for him. I called him one night and pleaded with him not to fight this particular battle. See, he'd fought so many battles, that this was just another fight with him. Few wanted to hear him or help him. While he lost the battle and left the district, our students experienced a bigger loss of no longer having access to an incredible educator and mentor. My father used to say, "Don't pick no battle you can't win." Us big idea people lean towards fighting too many battles which diminishes our ability to fight altogether. When I feel the need to advocate for something, I have to remind myself of my teacher friend.

There are so many of us who become the bottlenecks in our own lives. I know I've heard a lot of people say, "I realized that I had to get out of my own way." We all get that phrase, right? I just think that when you don't think like everybody else in the room, you are more likely to come up with great ideas that can have big impact. We have the problem of having too many ideas, so we can get overloaded, burn people out and become less effective at moving ideas forward. By intentionally de-bottlenecking ourselves, we give ourselves a higher likelihood of success. I want that for you, for me, and for our world.

SELF REFLECTIONS

1. How do bright, shiny objects distract you?

2. How can you create a filter for what ideas you will follow and which ones you'll let go?

3. What kind of people can you partner with to improve the number of ideas that come to fruition?

CHAPTER FIVE.
THE WORLD NEEDS YOUR IDEAS

"Great things are NOT accomplished by those who yield to trends and fads and popular opinion."

JACK KEROUAC

W hen I was in high school, my father shared with me his expectation for "smart" people. He said that they are obligated to go into the hard sciences since those subjects require more brain power in his estimation. While I don't think he was quite right on his expectation and I don't like to obligate anyone to anything, I do feel that out-of-the-box thinkers can be a real force for change and I want them to see themselves in that light. I want the people who don't think like everyone else in the room to challenge the status quo, ask the tough questions and make waves.

Sore Thumb

If you have ideas that are edgy and bold, you may not want to voice them for fear of sticking out like a sore thumb. What if people judge you?

What if your idea is dumb? What if nobody supports you? It's easier to keep your thoughts to yourself than to stick your neck out. However, easier isn't the goal. Sometimes we have to take risks in order to achieve and succeed.

One of my clients, Cal, was struggling with his business when he sought my services. He was insecure about his ability to grow and worried about all the bad things that might befall him if he exposed his different ideas. Cal was playing small, and he knew he had bigger goals inside of him. His challenge was his fear of things like not being good enough or being judged and rejected.

During our work together, Cal discovered that his work brought people out of significant pain and into relief. In a few cases, the impact was he saved people from wanting to die. This was powerful work, yet it was a challenge for him to own it. Even when I stated the fact that he had saved people's lives, he got all "aww shucks" on me. I persisted until he owned his power. Once he accepted that reality, he was able to admit that he must cast a wider net. He believed that people needed him to do his work, and he was able to start upping his professional game. He asked for meetings with high level folks in industries where he felt he could do the most good. While he was uncomfortable with playing a bigger game, he continued to do it and accepted the risks. Once he owned the power of his work, he was able to stick his neck out and tolerate the discomfort.

When he was hemming and hawing over connecting with high level decision makers, I gave him a visualization that really resonated for him. I said to imagine himself in the desert carrying a huge jug of water. There are people everywhere who are dehydrated and thirsty. They desperately need water. Instead of providing them water, he was putting his hand up and saying, "Sorry, I don't think I'm good enough yet, so you'll just have to wait." When the work is important and impactful, dare I say it, I want you to feel obligated to share it with the world. Yep, it's scary. Sure, you'll get kicked around. Uh-huh, people will judge, reject, scoff at and ignore you. Do it anyway. The world is full of thirsty people and you may be the one person carrying the water.

Curiouser and Curiouser

When you don't think like everyone else, you probably have an inclination to be curious about most things. When most people accept things as a given, you get curious. You ask seemingly obvious questions and find that there aren't easy answers. This usually leads to even more questions for you, which is fascinating and energizing. People like you are the ones that can lead people to find better solutions. The beauty of curiosity is that it doesn't come from a place of judgment. I have a scar on my back that is large and kinda ugly. When a small child asks, "What's that?" I don't feel judged. In the same way, when out-of-the-box thinkers get curious, they are coming from a place of wonder and interest.

One of my clients, Sue, runs a training company. She was always curious about the way we address health in this country. She experienced all sorts of issues related to health, and she was befuddled and disappointed by the system. When she started the get curious about how professionals approach health, she discovered that she had lots of ideas that hadn't been tried yet. Instead of waiting for the health industry to change, she decided to launch a business that addressed health in a totally different way. When Sue works with an organization, she gently but persistently questions everything they are doing. To Sue, there are no givens. By the time she's finished, each group is left with superior, more creative solutions.

Another example includes the big push to expand Science, Technology, Engineering and Math (STEM) programs in the world of education and economic development. Most people will agree that STEM careers are lucrative and important. They provide solid careers for our citizens, as well as products and services we want and need. STEM is good, check. Now, if you listen closely, you'll hear the brave souls who challenge this given about STEM being an obvious "good" thing. They are advocating for the Arts to be brought into the equation, going from STEM to STEAM. These folks are challenging how we can innovate if we don't have people in the system who think differently. I love this approach, because it challenges the status quo, promotes curiosity and debate about the STEM movement and creates better ideas with better results.

Interrupting Group Think

We all like to be around likeminded individuals who think like us. I know I experience a lot of energy when I am with people like me. However, I think there is a distinction between people who are likeminded and group think. Group think occurs when everyone in the group goes along with the popular idea to fit in and not rock the boat. They will justify this behavior by telling themselves that if everyone else thinks this idea is good, then it must be good. Who am I to disagree? On the other hand, being in a group of likeminded individuals allows for debate and discussion where alternative ideas can be considered and you won't be excluded from the group as a result of your different ideas. Out-of-the-box thinkers are well versed in interrupting group think.

My coach, Rich Litvin, gave me a great idea. In an effort to surround himself with really interesting people, he started "Interesting People" dinners. He invites five to ten of the most interesting people he knows to gather together over a meal and connect. I stole his idea and assembled people who I thought were doing amazing work in both their businesses and communities. They were all from different industries, so I called it "Pollinator Dinners", where people who might not come together could cross pollinate their ideas. My hope was that bringing five to ten remarkable people and putting them in the same room would yield something good, awesome and worthwhile. I was right!

My Pollinator Dinners are rife with debate. We discuss all sorts of different issues. We challenge each other and conventional wisdom. We toss out crazy and unconventional ideas. It's like watching a verbal tennis match, where one person's comment leads to another person's idea which leads to yet another person's even better idea, and so on. By the time I leave, my body is humming in positive energy. These are the people who help to elevate each other's ideas, become more creative in their approaches and find the courage and confidence to play a bigger game.

If you are an out-of-the-box thinker, then you may be reticent to interrupt an idea that is gaining momentum in the room. The goal is improving upon already great ideas. If we are going to upset the apple cart, then it'd help if there is a payback.

It's Okay That You Don't Fit In

If you are an out-of-the-box kind of thinker, then you may not fit in with most people. If you are like me, you've hidden your different thinking so that you wouldn't stand out. When we question things that have been accepted for long periods of time, we might face opposition. It's hard to see that your different thoughts are anything but a liability if you are constantly being shut down or rejected. After spending most of my adult life hiding my thinking, I'm here to say that it is actually a gift.

People don't like to be challenged on their beliefs. When we question or get curious, some people become defensive. You may be met with negative comments or behaviors, which can lead you to believe that you should keep your ideas to yourself. Although counterintuitive, your different thinking is a gift to these folks. They may be defensive in the moment, but those ideas or questions that you proposed will marinate in their minds. They will bounce around inside their heads shifting their perspective. In this way, you've given them a gift that keeps giving.

Let's use an example. When I realized that my husband was an alcoholic, I figured that the only solution was divorce. That's a given, right? What self-respecting woman would stay married to a dysfunctional person and allow her children to witness this behavior? I sought out an Alanon group, where friends and family members of alcoholics find support. Of course, I went with the intention of finding the magic solution to fixing my husband's drinking problem. Instead, I received a piece of advice that pissed me off but proved to be a beautiful solution. I was lamenting about how I was going to get the divorce process started, and how I was so busy at work, and how I was barely managing to parent my two toddlers. I was distraught and stressed, lost and frantic. One of the older members calmly said, "Honey, no decision is a decision." In my self-righteous anger and resentment, this statement just exacerbated my anxiety. No decision? Was she crazy? I HAD to make a decision so I could move forward. I NEEDED to have an answer. Just tell me what to do, please!

For weeks, that statement gnawed at me. The conventional wisdom was to kick him out, get a good attorney and create a list of assets to be split up. This woman challenged that wisdom with one simple statement. Her different thought made me uncomfortable, and it wouldn't go away. There was some part of me that wanted to understand what it meant and how it could be true. Because if it was true, then I could take some of the pressure off of myself to pick a path. She was essentially saying that I was at a fork in the road and that I didn't HAVE to choose a path. I could stay at the fork and be in the space of indecision, which ironically is a decision. So. Much. Weight. Lifted.

Thankfully, my husband did find recovery and has been sober for close to a decade. We stayed married. We faced our challenges. We grew as individuals and as a couple. We kept our family intact. I learned that not thinking like everyone else saved both me and my marriage. I no longer want or need to fit in most places, like with the ranks of the divorced single moms. Instead, I want to find deep belonging with a few people, like with my Alanon family. When I can give up the desire to fit in, then I can share my unconventional thoughts, beliefs, and ideas. By not fitting in, I have found more belonging.

Having Impact

At the end of the day, most of us want to have impact. We can put up with all sorts of terrible conditions if we believe we are making a difference. The trick is to know when we need to step up and when we can let things go. As an out-of-the-box thinker, I can get myself worked up into a lather about most issues. The real struggle is to identify the issues I feel so strongly about that I am willing to do things that make me uncomfortable. These are the moments when I have to summon my courage because the people pleaser in me hates making waves and just wants everyone to feel good. When I buck the system, I better be ready for the fallout, which isn't always pleasant.

I was meeting with a prospective client the other day, Nate, who is on the leadership team of a large medical services company. He said something to me that struck me. He wanted to transform the culture of his organization, but he didn't really want to put in a lot of effort and energy if nothing was going to change anyways. That's what Nate said. All

I heard was, "What if I fail?" Nate didn't want to try hard, stick his neck out, expose his ideas and launch new initiatives if nothing would change. Makes sense. Well, one thing I know for sure, nothing changes if nothing changes. Profound, I know.

We discussed what Nate wanted for the organization. He described the ideal environment that he would love to enter each day. He got excited when he talked about how he saw the organization not as it is, but what it could be. We used this vision as the foundation for his work ahead. When he didn't feel like going against the grain, he would remind himself that he was ready to position himself and his organization on a different trajectory. In order to achieve the new vision, Nate will have to put up with the voice in his head that tells him to cool it, let someone else do that work, and hide his big, bold ideas. He agreed to gently pat that voice on the head and thank it for wanting to protect him. By acknowledging and being aware of his fears, Nate has begun the journey of becoming more courageous.

I remember Sean Stevenson, the motivational speaker, once said that he became courageous by doing things that scared him. If we have big, bold ideas that challenge the status quo, then these ideas will probably be met with resistance. In order to overcome that resistance, we need to conquer the fears that have us hiding what we think and want we do. I truly believe that my work is to unlock out-of-the-box thinkers so they can go out and do their meaningful work because the world needs more of what these types of people have to give. Look, we don't think like everyone else in the room, so we may get hammered when we share our thoughts. But our different thinking is a gift, and we can share that gift if we accept that the path may be uncomfortable and risky and unconventional and different and wonderful and beautiful and powerful. We have enough people who are okay with hiding. I hope you aren't one of them.

SELF REFLECTIONS

1. What stops you from saying something that you know will make others uncomfortable?

2. How has your curiosity benefitted you, your family and your professional life?

3. How do you deal with fear?

CHAPTER SIX.
THE WORLD DESPERATELY NEEDS PEOPLE LIKE US

"The one single factor that determines society's success is the percentage of change-makers within it."

BILL DRAYTON

live in a small town in northeastern Wisconsin. Not much happens here. Recently, I had the opportunity to go to an entrepreneur's event at Lambeau Field (Go Pack Go!). They limited the participants and speakers to within an 80-mile radius. These folks came together to share and speak about their innovative programs, missions, and movements. As I mingled amongst the people who were solving hunger, providing affordable, clean energy to Africa, and offering abused women reliable transportation and the means to make a living wage, I realized these were the very people for whom this book is written. I have also come to believe that the world desperately needs people like us.

The Big Challenge

Society runs well when its people conform to the rules. However, sometimes the rules need a nudge. The people who do the nudging are the ones who see how things can be better and have the passion to present their ideas to the masses. These are usually people who see the world differently, and they are a valuable resource. If you are reading this book, then I suspect there is a part of you that resonates with the person who sees things differently, notices how things could be better, and says, "It doesn't have to be that way."

The big challenge is finding the courage to challenge the status quo. At this point, I'd like to speak to the leader in you. This is the part of you that wants to go against the grain. This is the part of you that is tired of watching people be treated badly by doing things the wrong way. This is the part of you that gets passionate about changing a system that no longer serves us. However, there are other parts of you that are fearful of, resistant to, or overwhelmed by taking on an extensive, immense mission. This internal conflict happens to all of us. Those of us that carry out the big mission in spite of these barriers are leaders.

When you think differently from everyone else in the room, it means you have lots of ideas, many of which haven't been thoroughly kicked around. These ideas, when you have the courage to present them, may have the potential to change the world in some way. We have enough managers. You know, the people who uphold the status quo and focus on more effective ways to get work done. What we need more of are leaders. Leaders start movements. Leaders promote change. Leaders do the things that rest of us are scared to do.

When we ask a group of people to consider a new idea or new way of thinking, they have to consider it and may find the process of reflection uncomfortable. They may feel the need to defend or justify not changing. After all, most humans resist change. We tend to get comfortable in our stability. Inertia takes over, and we need a prod to get the momentum to move in a different direction. Great ideas and great passion can provide that push if we can be brave enough to expose them to each other.

Shift Perspective

To experience personal, professional, emotional, and spiritual growth, we have to change our perspective. Even a one-degree shift can unlock us from some of the underlying beliefs that have held us back. Consider a plane. For every one degree a plane is off the correct heading, the plane will be off course by about 100 feet. This means that a one-degree shift can have you missing the mark by about a mile for every sixty miles a plane flies. Just a one-degree shift can have you end up at a totally new endpoint. How does this relate to mindset? This is good news for us humans because it means if can slightly shift our thoughts, then we will experience immense results. Because we are the people who think differently, we have the ability to shift people's thinking just by sharing what we are thinking. This is both a responsibility and a gift.

I have a client who challenges communities to shift how we work with our youth in a dramatically different way. He had this sense that we were handling things poorly, and the data support his hypothesis. So he decided to do the courageous thing and challenge all of us. He has created a movement that is ruffling feathers. He keeps going anyway. He has people telling him that he's wrong. He keeps going anyway. He gets rejected on a regular basis. He keeps going anyway. As he is moving forward, everyone who witnesses his movement is forced to shift how they think, even if it's just for a moment. We are all growing as a result.

When the youth are getting better as a result of his work, it is harder for us to shift back to our old way of thinking.

Another client of mine was struggling with an employee. This client has been running her business for over 20 years, so she was pretty confident that she knew what the problem was with her employee. She shared with me that this was a millennial who was just lazy. Because I am a different thinker, I got curious and asked if there were other reasons that this employee seemed incapable of getting his work done on time and to their standards. I told her to give me any options that came to mind. Just throw out ideas and see what happens. This exercise immediately shifted her perspective. She had to change how she was looking at him to answer my question. In less than five minutes, she came to realize that she had created a corporate culture that made it impossible to ask for help and admit when you don't know something. By shifting her perspective, she was able to uncover the real cause of her employee's problems and better assist him in getting what he needs to succeed.

If you don't think like anyone else in the room, then you can be the catalyst for a shift in perspective. For me, coaching is only one way to facilitate a shift in how a person looks at the world. Challenging the status quo is another way. Staring movements is yet another. That shift, regardless of how it occurred, causes growth. When we grow, we learn, we improve, and we get better.

Evolved Thinkers

I think of a highly evolved thinker as someone who has strong self-awareness, self-acceptance, and self-regulation. To get to this level of evolution, most of us have to go through multiple experiences that result in personal growth and development. It might look like breakdowns followed by breakthroughs. It may be going through a particularly challenging situation where a person is forced to go in a different direction. It could be ending up in a dark hole emotionally or spiritually and finding that a new mindset is the way out. For some reason, discomfort seems to be part of the process of evolving how we think.

As we participate in the journey of continuous discovery, we are able to let go of some of the less evolved thinking behind. Here is where the real value starts to emerge because this is where we come to understand more profound meanings in life. For example, the less evolved thinking of love is an if-then proposition. If you ask me to marry you, then you love me. If you help with the children, then you love me. If you quit drinking, then you love me. Lots of expectations, both spoken and unspoken, live in the world of if-then, conditional love. It's also where most of our relationships can stall out if we aren't careful.

A higher evolution of love is unconditional love. It means we experience love regardless of what the other person does or says or believes. Unconditional love is relieved of the burden of expectations, which makes it easier to experience. This opens us up to loving more people more deeply. People who think differently have a high capacity for discovery, which makes them prime for highly evolved thinking. When they can ascend to higher evolutions of thinking, their ideas become more meaningful as well. Developing an evolved sense of consciousness is a gateway to a happier, more productive life.

I have a client who started with me at an average level of thinking. He had done just enough work on his own to know that there were higher states of satisfaction and purpose, but he was stalled out. He was getting stuck in worrying about how he was being perceived, rather than working on understanding himself more intensely. The visual I have in my mind is of this client holding out a mirror to everyone and asking if HE looked okay. Our work together had him turning the mirror back at himself.

During a session, he was agonizing about feeling so tired from trying to take care of everyone. We explored how solving other people's problems served him. His big insight happened when he realized that fixing was satisfying him, but didn't really help anyone else. This is when something inside him clicked. He was able to decouple caring about someone and fixing them. The weight was immediately lifted. When he practiced loving people without having to fix their problems or give them solutions, he could love more people more deeply. By growing his self-awareness, his thinking reached a higher level of evolution which paid off big dividends in his relationships.

Growth Mindset

Carol Dweck introduced us to the "growth mindset" in her book *Mindset* published in 2006. The idea is that we can learn and grow as much as we want because we are not innately born with traits that we are locked into for life. A growth mindset supports our neuroplasticity. We know that our minds are constantly learning and adjusting. We are lucky because we can consciously decide the mindset we want to have. If we want to believe that people are just wired to be smart, athletic, thin, funny, etc., then we have a closed mindset. If we choose to believe that anything is possible and there is always a way to get what we want, then we have a growth mindset.

People who think differently usually have a growth mindset. They are a curious group who are continuously looking for a different way. These folks are thirsty to learn, and most of my clients learn through experience. Their growth mindset helps them to take risks, fail without judgment and reflect on what they have learned. Lots of experiences results in lots of learning.

My daughter is a teenager, and she has plenty of intense experiences that have forced her to grow. Some people would characterize her as having a fair share of hard knocks, but that isn't how she sees it. Her perception is that the difficulties she faces have taught her how to cope at a younger age than most. She doesn't see that she was born a certain way or a victim of genetics. Instead, she has figured out that she can determine the best answers for herself and her solutions might not be the same as anyone else's.

For example, she has plenty of drama with her middle school peers. With social media, it seems much more intense than I ever experienced at her age. One night, she was caught up in a group chat that became a heated argument between two groups of young ladies. She became stressed and worried, and found it difficult to sleep. She asked me if she could take a mental health day the following day to regroup. I'm not sure that most teens would know to ask for a mental health day. Even if they did, I wonder how many parents would agree. Our daughter made her case without any excuses, blaming or victim talk. She knew she had gone too far and things had gotten emotional. She deleted the app. She blocked some people on her mobile device. She took a day to lay low, read a book, snuggle with her pets and reflect on what had happened. This is how a growth mindset approaches challenges and learns from them.

One of my colleagues is in a wheelchair. At coffee the other day, he shared with me that he doesn't care if he fails. He has a degenerative nerve disorder, so he had to learn at a young age that he may literally fall on his face without warning. He decided that he wasn't going to make that a big deal. His growth mindset allowed him to overcome the humiliation and embarrassment that could accompany falling in front of people. When I do something that is new and scary, I think of my friend and decide not to care if I stumble, make a mistake or mess things up.

Just Try It

I was talking with a colleague who used to teach teenagers. He is an innovative person who thinks differently from most teachers. He shared that he was always trying out lots of crazy ideas with his students. Other teachers would approach him and ask where he gets his ideas, how he gets great partners from the community to help out and how he gets his students to buy into what he's doing. His simple answer was "I just try it." After many, many trials, he would have some great breakthroughs that would lead to new trials and newer breakthroughs. Trying it is an effective approach to learning what works for you.

NPR has a podcast called "Invisibilia". One episode, titled "Flip the Script", detailed how the Danish police approached the problem of young Muslims being radicalized and running away from Denmark to travel to ISIS training camps. The police chose to flip the script from demonizing these youth to opening their hearts and bringing these young Muslims into the Danish community. They didn't know if it would work. They didn't know what they were doing. They just had an idea and they tried it. They learned as they went, and they tweaked as needed. They were able to reduce the numbers of young Muslims leaving Denmark to join terrorist groups and the ones that returned to Denmark have stayed and are part of the community.

There are many barriers that can get in the way of trying things. For example, I have been dreaming of a program for middle school kids that would have them loving themselves rather than tearing each other apart. When I shared this dream with others, I didn't get much support until I talked with Chris. My dream resonated with her too. We'd meet for coffee to brainstorm ideas to get a program up and running, but nothing would ever come of it. There were too many unknowns, and we couldn't quite get ourselves to the point where we could even get started. It wasn't until we broke the program into the tiniest step we needed to move forward that we got any traction at all. We agreed to work with two kids for a few hours for two Sundays in a row. It was small enough that it was doable. We could try it. We could tweak it. We could learn from it. Trying it took our dream and converted it into a reality.

Of course, trying it isn't easy because there are always going to be barriers. Here are a few of the barriers kept me stuck with my middle school dream.

- What will people think?
- What if the kids hate it?
- What if we can't find a location?
- What if someone gets hurt?
- What if it takes too much of my time?
- How will we be able to charge for it?
- What if nobody signs up?
- What will we learn if we only have 2 kids for two days?
- What if it fails?

See, I can keep on going because, frankly, I'm a marvelous catastrophizer. So the barriers never stop. It's just that I take the barriers, put them in a nice little compartment in the back of my brain and take the tiniest step that moves me closer to my goal. I know that trying it will teach me something because I've already decided that it will. The biggest risk is to do nothing or to not learn from trying it.

We all admire people who have big successes and have accomplished enormous goals. What we don't always realize is what it takes to get there.

Many of the change makers of today suffered through loads of failures, tons of fears and lots of rejections. They aren't so different from the rest of us. We may put them on a pedestal, but it only serves to make audacious goals unachievable for us. The world needs more change, more challenge, and more service. It needs us, the different thinkers, to step forward and share our ideas with others.

SELF REFLECTIONS

1. How can you be less like a manager and more like a leader?

2. How much time do you spend with people who have a growth mindset?

3. How will you overcome the barriers that stop you from trying out your new ideas?

CHAPTER SEVEN.
DON'T HIDE, NO MASK

"Sometimes it's not the people who change. It's the mask that falls off."

HARUKI MURAKAMI

I f I can accomplish just one thing in my life it would be to have everyone stop hiding who they are. We spend so much energy putting on a different face depending on who we surround ourselves with.

Honestly, how much time and resources do we devote to preserving our reputations and tucking away our limitations where they can't be seen? There are so many better and more deserving ways to realize and use our talents, skills or vision.

The Stress of Hiding

When we put our best selves on the outside regardless of how we are feeling on the inside, we are creating an internal conflict. When we are inauthentic, out of alignment and not in integrity, stress occurs. While stress can be an effective motivator, there is no question that too much stress can ruin our mental, spiritual and physical health.

After spending a good portion of my adult life hiding from who I was, I can attest to the deleterious effects of the stress on me, my family, my work and my wellness. I spent my life as an engineer for mostly the wrong reasons. The story begins in my childhood where I learned that I needed to think like everyone else in order to belong. My fear of abandonment was/is very strong, so it wasn't safe for me to be different. The conflict of thinking differently from everyone else had to be hidden away. In math and science, I could get the same answers as everyone else, like $1+1 = 2$ and $E=mc^2$, which meant I could fit in, which meant I could belong, which meant I wouldn't be abandoned. The theory was:

Get the same answer -> Be liked -> Fit in -> Belong ->
Never be abandoned

Which simplified into:

Get the same answer = Never be abandoned

Engineering offered me other things too, like status and a hefty salary. I could buy a beautiful home, drive nice cars, go on lovely vacations, you know the drill. Once again, I could get the same answer as everyone else, like the Joneses. It was all very logical and rational, except for the fact that I am a person who always wants to learn more about me and others as well. I thrive on connecting deeply with people. I had to ignore this gift. I had to push back my desire to have satisfying relationships. I had to douse my internal fire for intimacy with a tribe of likeminded individuals. So as long as I could dupe myself, the engineering gig could go on in perpetuity.

It only took me about 12 years of living this lie before I had made a complete mess of things. The way I look at it, when I pushed my me-ness down, the very core of me, it came out sideways. I became an insatiable people pleaser. I said yes to everything. I wasn't getting the belonging I was desperate for in the engineering world, so I sought it elsewhere. I became the sole caretaker of my terminally ill grandparents. I became my mother's go-to person for all problems, issues, and complaints. I took on all responsibility for my marriage, controlling every aspect of it. I spent countless hours doting on my children and ensuring they were taking advantage of the same opportunities as the kids I was reading about on my friend's Facebook pages. So if I throw in a night school MBA program into the mix, you can easily forecast how I was heading for a resounding crash.

And crash I did. My marriage ran into the ditch. I resented my family for not helping me with my grandparents, which resulted in several estrangements with people I loved. I was an impatient and temperamental mother, so my children never felt fully secure. I became sick easily and seemed to catch every cold, flu and bug. I developed a troubling drinking habit as a coping mechanism. I was forced to look at myself when I developed pneumonia and could not recover. My body had been trying to tell me all along that I was not well. The stress was taking its toll, but I ignored it. It wasn't until I went to the doctor and she remarked on my haggard appearance, thank you very much. After listening to my rattling lungs and asking how long I'd been suffering, she put a hand on my knee and kindly said, "You HAVE to slow down." With tears streaming down my face, all I felt was fear and shame.

Stress was a signal that I was running from something. When forced to see the mess I'd made, the emotional discomfort was huge. My natural inclination would have been to get back to what I knew, which was to be busy and stay busy, no matter what. Busy is a great distraction. Busy prevents me from facing my feelings. Busy doesn't ask me to reflect, to determine who I am, to change my behavior, thoughts or emotions. Busy has me running and doing and pretending I am important. Yet busy was the very thing that destroyed my relationships, my health and my ability to feel relaxed or peaceful.

We all know that our minds are physically attached to our bodies, so it shouldn't be surprising when stress in one part affects the other. Our minds and bodies are amazing, and they can truly handle much more than we think. It's the ongoing and unmitigated stresses that slowly break us down over time, like erosion. Hiding who I was caused internal conflict which caused continuous stress. Over time, that stress accumulated and I suffered greatly. When I stopped denying who I was, the suffering stopped too.

Maximum Operating Capacity

Since I stopped running from who I am, I've noticed a significant increase in my motivation, wellness, and peacefulness. When I had to hide my flaws, cover up my mistakes and keep up with the Joneses, I was depleted. When I get to showcase my strengths, live in alignment with who I am and make decisions based on what is important to me, I never seem to run out of energy. I like to call this my maximum operating capacity (MOC). Instead of dreading my day each morning, I get out of bed looking forward to that work I have planned. I giggle when I create mind-blowing proposals for my clients. I sometimes shake a little during a coaching session because there is a lot of energy surging through my body. There are times when I literally think my heart might just burst with how much I love my life. Being at MOC serves me better. It serves my family, my business and my community in a more desirable and valuable way.

Zappo's, the shoe company, offers its employees a quitting bonus. I love this idea because it is grounded in the theory that you are no good to the company if you aren't operating at your MOC. If you don't thrive at Zappo's then that is okay. They'll pay you to leave so you can move on to find a place that suits you better. And they can find someone who does belong there. Just like at Zappo's, if you are dreading your job, your next family get-together or your next meeting with your community organization, then you are of little service to them. If you aren't at MOC, then recognize it is data for you to consider what isn't working for you.

There is a simple yet powerful exercise that my coach, Rich Litvin, uses. It's called an energy audit, where I identify the things in my life that drain me of energy and things that give me an energy boost. Below is an example.

Energy Gain +	Energy Drain -
Spending time with my husband and chidlren	Talking about parenting with my mother in law
Walking my dog	Inputting expenses for my business
Having a great session with a client	Saying yes to something I don't want to do

Notice that the things that give me energy are experiences when I can be myself. On the energy drain side, I have to hide who I am or operate outside of my strengths zone to do those things. Because life isn't all puppy dogs and rainbows, the goal of the energy audit isn't to eliminate the things that drain our energy. Rather it is to minimize them and create ways to be at peace when you have to do them.

For instance, my mother-in-law has very deeply held beliefs that she wants me to value and accept as my own. Her beliefs work well for her but they don't work well for me. We are at an impasse. Therefore, when we visit, I have to find ways to minimize the energy drain that it takes on me. I find that by setting clear boundaries for myself, I can bypass debates where neither of us gets what we want. As I practice keeping my boundaries, I have improved my confidence to be with my mother-in-law without being hurt by her comments and opinions. This, naturally, leads to a pathway for us to not just tolerate each other, but to get closer in other ways. While we may never agree on religion, child rearing and politics, I can still experience moments of joy when we are together. Energy drain minimized.

Do You Really Belong?

If you have to put on a mask to belong, then that seems like a terrible life sentence to me. Belonging based on who you are is much more powerful than fitting in because you know how to play the game. As a social chameleon who can expertly fit in anywhere, I found it painfully ironic that I never felt like I was a part of the group. In fact, I had a coach once remark at my ability to not just fit in, but to match the intelligence of the people I was around so I could get the same answer thereby avoiding abandonment. He coined the term "equi-telligence". It wasn't until put down my mask that I experienced a sense of belonging.

Burnout

Many of my initial coaching conversations have been with people who describe themselves as burned out. They say they're exhausted and sick of the work they do. They feel unfulfilled and dissatisfied. When we dive a little deeper, I discover that many of these folks have spent a lot of time and energy learning how to play the game, how to get things done and how to grease the skids for future work needs. In short, they figured how to bend and twist to fit into a system that doesn't fulfill them.

I had several conversations with a potential client who had taken on a job that was outside of her comfort zone. She was ready for a challenge, and this opportunity seemed to emerge at just the right time. However, 6 months into this new gig, she was insecure, losing sleep and putting on weight at a rapid pace. As she worked harder and harder to fit in, she became more and more stressed. Her assumption was that she needed to be "like" everyone else to get her initiatives achieved. Instead of being herself, admitting to what she didn't know and focusing on her strengths, she put on a professional mask each day to hide who she was and how she thought. It only served to make her job more difficult and her performance less effective. While we didn't end up working together, I always hoped she would find a way to take off that mask. I suspect that if she did, she could have improved her ability to do her job and re-align herself with who she is in the world, not to mention recover her confidence and physical health.

True Belonging = Deep Connection

We, humans, have an intense need for belonging that we can blame on our evolution. Our very survival depended on our ability to be part of a tribe. When we are part of a clan, crew or community, we experience deep and meaningful connections with others. If we can put down the masks we wear to fit in, then we can find the place in this world we are truly meant to be.

Not only did I develop all sorts of masks as a child, teen and young adult, but I found an irresistible one when I became a mother. When I had children, I became obsessed with how I was perceived. When I shopped and my children started crying or throwing a tantrum, I would leave lest someone think I'd lost control of my kids. When my kids played in puddles and got dirty, I was quick to clean them off lest someone think I was neglectful. When my kids had certain behavioral issues, I swiftly swept them under the rug lest someone think my kids picked up that behavior at home.

When my son was in elementary school, he was having a difficult day and had hit his limit. In a moment of emotional frustration and panic, he screamed out that he wanted to kill himself. Later that day, when I arrived at school to pick him up, several of his classmates ran up to me to tell me what had happened. After all, there is nothing like a 4th grader with juicy gossip. My first thought was how could he do such a thing? He was embarrassing me. When he emerged, he was visibly distraught. With my teeth clenched, I leaned down and told him to get himself together and go straight to the car. I still remember the hurt and betrayed look on his face. Just when he needed his mommy to scoop him into a hug and tell him he will be okay, I dismissed his needs and tried to shuttle him to a place where I could hide his embarrassing behavior. I was mortified at what the teachers would think. About me. I worried about what his classmates would tell their parents. About me. I wondered if the school counselor would call me to discuss his behavior. Notice how none of these concerns were focused on the well-being of my son. By focusing on what others would think of my mothering, I was ignoring the one person who made me a mother in the first place.

When I wore those masks, I put up walls in my relationships. My son learned that I didn't have his back, which surely didn't bring us closer.

When I put down the masks and decided to do what was right for him, our relationship deepened. We became very close, and he eventually learned that he could trust me to be there for him no matter what. Once I accepted the kind of mother I wanted to be, I no longer needed the acceptance of teachers, other parents or counselors. After all, they didn't know me or my son and what we needed. Their judgments no longer held any weight.

Honor Thyself

We really can be our own worst enemy. When we don't honor who we are and what we are on this planet to do, we risk not fully experiencing life. It is darn near impossible to honor others if we can't do it for ourselves. If we are more concerned with judging someone so we can file them in some preconceived category, i.e. know-it-all, bad mother, self-absorbed, then we aren't open to experiencing other parts of them that may be of great joy or service to us. Haven't you ever formed an opinion about a person and come to find out that you were way off base? Haven't you ever thought of yourself in a certain way and found out you were wrong? The beauty in honoring who you are is that you can finally let go of all the "should-ing" on yourself, which is great because then you don't "should" on others either. It's incredibly freeing. If you "should" on yourself and others, I invite you to try going one week without using the word "should" and see what you discover.

I have a client who used judgment as a way to avoid connecting with others. Not surprisingly, she was quite a harsh judge of herself. She had been denying who she is for a long time. When she would share with me what really got her excited, it was clear that she knew who she was. As we would continue to move towards letting her true self shine, she would immediately become concerned with what other people would think.

By not honoring herself, she wasn't honoring others and was unable to move forward. When she began accepting herself and her mission in the world, she started to come out of her cave. She found others more enjoyable to be around. She found ways to like people she previously judged. She deepened her family relationships. Her business started to become attractive to the people who needed her work in the world. She definitely broke the cycle, experienced professional success and deepened her connection to others.

If you are unsure about who you are and unclear how to start that journey, then please understand there is no workbook, theoretical model or well defined means to get there. We all arrive at different points in our lives from different motivations using different tools and strategies. Just try something new. Lean into your discomfort. Challenge yourself. My hope is that we are always on a quest to learn more about ourselves so we can stop hiding. Let's use our energy to create something incredible instead.

SELF REFLECTIONS

1. What indications do you have that you are hiding parts of yourself from the world?

2. What are 3 things you can do to approach your Maximum Operating Capacity (MOC)?

3. What is the payoff for having deep, meaningful connections with others?

CHAPTER EIGHT.
YOU KNOW YOU BELONG WHEN...

*"Fitting in is about assessing a situation and becoming
who you need to be accepted. Belonging, on the other hand,
doesn't require us to change who we are."*

BRENE BROWN

B elonging is critical for us to feel safe, secure and cared for. Is belonging a feeling? What does it feel like? How will I know when I have true belonging? What is the difference between belonging and fitting in? Let's take a look at what it looks like to find true belonging.

Warts and All?

When you can take off your mask and be yourself without fear of being judged, then you probably belong. Ironically, there are groups of people that are so judgmental that part of how they create belonging is by judging others together, like religious groups, athletics, and country clubs. Just look at many of today's social media posts, and you will find no shortage of judgments and opinions hurled about. If I am desperate enough, I will tolerate this behavior. I call this the middle school model of belonging. You may experience momentary shots of being a part of a group, but you still have to hide parts of yourself to be in. This is fitting in, not belonging.

I used to LOVE gossiping. I could fit in very quickly and easily when I could find just one other person who enjoyed speaking badly about other people. If you don't have something nice to say, then come sit next to me. We'd whisper and giggle and make rude comments. We'd judge. We'd have strong opinions. We'd "should" on people. The rub was that I always felt badly afterward. I secretly wondered if someday someone would overhear me or catch me on video saying terrible things. I was completely out of integrity when I gossiped, and I knew it. We are motivated to gossip from our fear of being lesser than, having low self-esteem and creating scapegoats. My mind could overpower my heart and my gut, but there was always this feeling of unease that I couldn't totally ignore. It always caught up with me. I was mistaking "fitting in" with belonging. If you can't have deep connection, then you probably don't have belonging.

It's one thing to know that you need to move away from certain groups of people. It's quite another to actually do it. I found it to be a painful process, as I had come to love many of these people even though I became uncomfortable with who I was when I was with them. The confidence to follow through with it came from the people in my life that accepted for who I am. When I began, I could count all the people who really knew me on one hand. Thankfully, these few people supported me as I allowed some people to drift out of my life.

What I Don't Want You To Know About Me

When I first joined a coaching group after 6 months of trying to launch my coaching business, I was expecting to learn the tips and tricks to make my business grow. So imagine my surprise when on our first video call, our coach asked us to introduce ourselves followed by the statement "what I don't want you to know about me is ..." Because I had no time to prepare an answer that would impress them or show how smart I am, I blurted out, "I don't want you to know that I don't think I belong here." Then our coach asked if anyone else felt the same way and raise their hands. Every one of those 9 other coaches raised their hand. I had shown a little bit of my vulnerability to these strangers, and they accepted me. I felt instant relief, connection, and love. Week after week, our video calls would have us sharing our vulnerabilities with each other. After spending 6 months with these people, my confidence exploded as I had a deep sense of belonging with a group of people who shared our darkest and scariest thoughts with each other. They didn't judge me. They didn't minimize my fears. They didn't avert their eyes when I made my ugly cry face. They didn't try to fix, rescue or save me. They just listened, connected and supported me. You know you belong when people accept you, warts and all.

Big Ideas OK?

As a person who experiences possibility-gasms™ from new ideas, I learned that finding the right idea people was critical. Suddenly, all of those people I used to make fun of for their pie in the sky ideas became my best resources. These people have remained the same, but I am the one who changed. When I need to brainstorm a new idea, these are the people who are incredibly valuable to me. Of course, I also become a resource for their big ideas. It's like a huge idea-love-excitement-possibility-gasm™ fest. Sharing an idea is a vulnerable, out on a limb act, so it is critical to find a group who will give you a safe space for it.

It's always seemed contradictory that we tend to dismiss people with crazy ideas, but we glamorize them if their ideas actually work, like Elon Musk, Abraham Lincoln, and Mahatma Gandhi. I have been on the school board for seven years. One of my fellow school board members has all sorts of ideas that are way outside of the box. Many of the status quo types get uncomfortable when he presents his big, bold ideas. Yet he never seems deterred. He would take the criticism, eye rolling and smirking and continue on his merry way. Next meeting, he would probe us with another what if question, and the idea would get shot down. Again. There was always a part of me that was inspired by his ideas and the way he tenaciously came back each time with another edgy thing to try.

When I decided to change careers, he was notably somebody I sought for support. I mean, really, who goes from 20 years of designing oil refineries to becoming a coach anyways. When he heard my idea, he loved it. He found all sorts of ways to love it. He supported it before it even came out of my mouth. I've continued to use him as a sounding board for my own crazy ideas, and it's been priceless to me and my business. When you have people with whom you can share your crazy ideas, then you have true belonging.

Looking Out For You?

When I was involved in groups, teams at work and different community organizations, I made the assumption that I belonged simply because I was a member. I was surrounded by other members, yet I still felt lonely. I think I have discovered another trait of true belonging has to do with intention. When someone is looking for my best interests, then I feel like I can conquer anything.

One of my female clients had some pretty serious marital issues. She and her husband were slipping into a downward spiral of resentment and anger. Years of unmet expectations, betrayals, financial mishandlings and verbal abuses left these two feel like there was no hope of building a bright future together. My client shared her feelings with her spouse one evening in a very effective way by using her "I" statements, asking open ended questions and trying desperately to be kind and curious while simultaneously not being a doormat. The conversation ended with her spouse leaving without any word on whether or not he was returning. While distraught, she was proud of herself for having a difficult conversation without losing herself in the drama. When she returned from work the next day, her spouse was sitting in her home office looking at the financial books she kept for their side business. He looked up at her and said, "I never realized how complicated all of this was." In that moment, they both experienced the sense that he was looking out for her. He wanted her to know that he was clueless about how much pressure she was experiencing. He didn't want that for her. His acknowledgment showed her that he wanted to support her and also wanted to know more. It was a launching point for them to co-create a future where they each considered the other continuously. You know you belong when you have their best interests at heart, and they have yours too.

Peak Behind the Kimono?

If you know Brene Brown, then you know that vulnerability is an important skill to living a wholehearted life. She has shown us through her research, her books and her TED talks that we can all stand to be a little more vulnerable. Of course, it's not to be vulnerable to everyone all the time. Instead, it's to find another trustworthy human and share what's going on for us on the inside. This may feel risky, so having some people standing with you, literally or figuratively, can give you the courage to do so.

My coach, Rich Litvin, was conducting a live webinar on building a coaching practice. He had accepted a question from one of the participants. Rich started to dig into the question with this student, and it was clear to all of us listening in that the student was not engaged in the conversation. You could hear him typing in the background, and he was slow to respond to Rich's questions. After a few minutes, Rich asked the guy to stop typing and give his full attention. I was stunned. It was exactly what I was thinking, but Rich actually said it. The guy stopped typing and agreed to get present with Rich.

Once the webinar was over, I sent a message to Rich acknowledging him for gently confronting that student about not being present during the webinar. I shared that it really landed with me because I have such difficulty calling people out their behavior. His reply was to let me see "behind the kimono". He told me that his team had instant messaged him that the guy was not really engaged. Rich said that even though he feared offending the guy, he decided to do the scary thing and ask him to be present. Rich acknowledged that it was super edgy for him.

When someone shares with you how scary something is for them, it helps you to find the courage to do the same thing. Courage is the result of doing scary stuff. Therefore, finding a tribe where you can discuss these fears and challenges is critical to being courageous. Being a part of Rich's community allows me to expose my vulnerabilities. You know you belong when you can feel safe to be vulnerable.

Love Me Unconditionally?

When I think of unconditional love, I immediately think of parenting. I didn't really understand what it meant to love someone unconditionally until I had children. The beauty of unconditional love is that you have to be able to love yourself unconditionally before you can offer it to anyone else. It also offers both opportunity and motivation to find a way to love yourself if you don't already.

When my kids came along, the intensity of the love I had for them confused me. There were times that I swear my heart hurt with how much I loved them. It was the reason that I wanted to be a better mother, better wife, and better person. I sought the help and support of people who would teach me to be kind to myself, to listen to the wise voice in my head and to accept myself fully. When I did this, my love for my children grew exponentially. By loving my whole self, I could give even more love to them.

I am in Alanon, which is a support group for friends and family members of alcoholics. It was in this group that I learned how to love people other than my children unconditionally. Week after week, I would attend the Alanon meetings. When people are impacted by their loved one's addiction, it is an agonizing place to be. Having a place to work through those emotions has the power to change people's lives. The beauty of Alanon is that we are a group of strangers who gather for a single reason. The structure of the program offers us a safe container.

One of the sentences that we read at each Alanon meeting is:

"While you may not like every one of us, you will learn to love each of us in a very special way, the same way we already love you."

Being a member of this group for years has shown me how to love unconditionally. When people hurt or betray me, I can still find a way to love them. It seems like because I can now do it, I attract others who can do it as well. The people I choose to hang out with can love me unconditionally, which offers a level of belonging that satisfies me in an almost primal way. You know you belong when you can love someone unconditionally and you can receive their unconditional love.

Have My Back?

As a child who was consistently let down by the people in my family, I learned very early that nobody had my back. It meant that I couldn't think about my own needs. I had to be willing to go with the flow. I couldn't ask for too much. I had to give way to what others wanted. It was too difficult to ask for what I wanted and be denied or rejected. I developed a way of being a low-maintenance friend and family member. If I didn't rock the boat, then I could be a part of the clan.

When I married at 25, I was adamant that I would never depend on my husband. I watched my mother, who was dependent upon my father, lose herself when they divorced. Throughout most of my life, she reminded me to be able to support myself so nobody could ever screw me over. With that in mind, I set about to take total control of my marriage. I purchased our first home. I was in charge of our finances. I determined whether or not we went on vacations, for how long and where. When the kids came, I went into hyper-control mode. I determined the schedules, where they went for day care, what they ate, how they were disciplined. Guess what? I secretly resented my husband for not stepping up and not taking more responsibility. How could he? I wouldn't let him. So my self-righteous victimhood continued.

When my daughter was 4 years old, I got into a car accident with her in the car. I rear ended the car in front of me sending him over the center line where he was struck head on by another car. It was awful. Neither of the other drivers was wearing a seat belt, so there were very significant injuries. A woman pulled over to help and called 911. She then came up to me and asked if she could call someone for me. At first, the question seemed ludicrous. Why would I need someone? I don't need anyone. It's how I've designed my life. In that moment, I felt a gentle nudging to consider her question. I thought maybe I'd give my husband the chance to be there for me. It was hard for me to ask him. What if he said he couldn't leave work? What if he said he would talk to me about when he got home from work? What if I wasn't important enough for him? Thankfully, he dropped everything and rushed to be with my daughter and me.

See, the whole reason I never asked for help is that many times I received a no. Rejection hurts. Not being important enough hurts. Not mattering hurts. It reinforces that nobody has my back. It motivated me to live a life where I never depended on anyone. I assumed that asking was the risky thing. But what was I risking by never asking?

From that moment forward, I started to ask my husband for more and more. Just show up for me. For us. He rose to the challenge and felt much more connected to me as a result. Now, we are completely interdependent upon each other and there is no question that he has my back and I have his. By modeling this behavior with our kids, they have learned to play the have your back game too. When we have big issues in our family, the four of us can count on each other. You know you belong when you have their back and they have yours.

What holds us back from belonging is fear, which can look like resistance. It is useful to explore where the resistance originates. For me, my resistance to taking off my mask so I could belong starts with my fear of rejection. This fear originated in my formative years where my requests for help did not get fulfilled. I was also taught that asking for help was weak. Instead, we just worked harder and muscled through. When I brought that mindset into my marriage, I didn't honor myself or my husband. If I had to ask for help, it meant I had to be vulnerable, which opened me up to rejection, which hurt like heck. I have clients who resist making more money, asking for help, letting go of control. Resistance is the wake-up call that there's something to overcome. There is some story where the resistance lives, and shining a light on it can uncover a lifelong struggle to be freed.

Here are six statements to help determine if we have true belonging.

1. You know you belong when people accept you, warts and all.

2. You know you belong when you can share your big, bold ideas without fear of being judged or scoffed at.

3. You know you belong when they have your best interests at heart and you have theirs.

4. You know you belong when you can feel safe to be vulnerable.

5. You know you belong when you can love them unconditionally and receive their unconditional love as well.

6. You know you belong when you can count on them and they can count on you.

SELF REFLECTIONS

1. Where do you have true belonging?

2. How is fitting in serving you?

3. What resistance comes up when you ask for help?

CHAPTER NINE.
COMPARISON

"No one can make you feel inferior without your consent."

ELEANOR ROOSEVELT

C omparison is something we do so naturally, that we may not even give it a second thought. The person with the most votes wins. The person with the fastest time wins. The person with the best grades wins. Our culture and society are built on how we compare ourselves to each other. Our entire capitalist economy is built on comparing products and services to choose the best fit for you. Comparison may be effective when buying a flat screen TV or giving a gold medal at a swim meet, but it's not always great at determining your worth as a parent, business person or human being.

Comparison has been baked into our cultural and emotional DNA. In today's American culture, we swipe left or swipe right after comparing two choices, for instance on Tinder where your worth is given a 3 second glance and a swipe on a screen. We have apps that comparison shop for us, desensitizing us to seeing all the pros and cons of each choice. We have internalized the urge to swipe left or right with lots of things, like what makes me feel good, who wore a dress better, or Would You Rather?

(WYR) smartphone games. Data shows us that the more time people spend on online media, the less happy they are. The theory is that online media encourages us to compare ourselves to the perfect portrayals we see on posts, and it leaves us ALL feeling less than.

Stops You in Your Tracks

When I went off to college, I was told to enroll in 18 credits, study hard and stay focused. I was a smart kid, they told me. I could handle it, they said. Since I had gotten good grades, scored well on standardized tests and graduated in the upper echelons of my class, I must be smart enough, right? Freshman chemistry stopped me in my tracks. I was in my dorm room with my roommate, who was taking the same class. She was blowing through the homework without any trouble at all, and I couldn't remember who Avagadro was and what his number was used to calculate. If my roommate was cruising through the homework without a single glitch, then I must be a real dummy. I lasted 3 semesters before withdrawing from the university, convinced that I was not smart enough to succeed.

I have a colleague, Joan, who owns well known business in our area. She has a great reputation, and her clientele is loyal and incredibly supportive. Joan told me that her business was no longer making money. She was considering closing up shop, but she had one issue. She imagined her closest competitor and nemesis scoffing at her. Joan compared her business to her competitor's, which can be useful and strategic but can also keep her from making the right decision. Joan is not her competitor. Joan doesn't know if her competitor is making money, and if so, how much. By holding herself up to her competitor, she is no longer making decisions based on what is best for her and her business.

Comparison lures our self-doubt from the shadows. It robs us of our essence and stops us in our tracks. I was and am smart enough to graduate engineering school, but when I compared myself to others in my program, I doubted myself and I quit. Comparison pounds away on our low confidence and makes it smaller and smaller and smaller. It's a subconscious leakage that can be repaired by avoiding comparison

Thief of Joy

Roosevelt said that comparison is the thief of joy. To anyone who has a Facebook account, we know how comparing ourselves to the picture-perfect images people post can really put a damper on our day. It seems like when my kids are imploding, I am suddenly and acutely aware of how everyone else's kids are heading off to Harvard, winning state championships and meeting the president. When I read these posts, I feel like a failure, like I'm not good enough, like I'm not doing it right. It's an energy drain.

Yes, yes, I know that these posts don't represent reality. These people have struggles too. They aren't perfect. But there is some part of my brain that gets revved up and starts telling me that I'd better start hustling more, raising higher achieving kids, and working harder on my abs and thighs. Here's the other thing I've learned. When I don't go on Facebook, I feel better about myself.

Enter Scott. He's in his 40's, works for a giant corporate conglomerate and has a family of four. He lives in a nice neighborhood, pays his taxes and votes in elections. He's done a lot of things he thought he was supposed to do, and yet he has begun to question if this is it. He has one foot out the door at his corporate job, because he realizes that he is not fulfilled in that organization. He wants to quit, but guess what is holding him back. He looks around and worries he won't be able to keep up with his peers. If he quits and has to move to a smaller house, then he thinks he's backsliding. If his family has to forgo luxury family vacations, then he worries his family will resent him when they have to listen to their friends brag about their trips to ski resorts and Caribbean all-inclusive resorts. He even feels anxious about his children's clothing and what might happen if they cannot afford designer brands.

Scott knows that intellectually all of his concerns are petty and completely surmountable. But he, too, has that little voice in his head that tells him to keep up with the Joneses. He is in the race and is afraid of what will happen if he walks off the track. So he continues to work at a job that is soul sucking so he can afford the amenities that has him staying neck to neck with his peers. After all, when he can tick off the boxes of tangible milestones, he is succeeding at the game. Except his definition of success is making him miserable.

What is Scott to do? We have created a plan for him to start moving towards a more enjoyable life. He is taking small steps towards that future, and he is finding that the comparison that holds him back is decreasing in intensity. He has learned to truly consider actions before taking them and questioning his purpose for doing them. For example, he built a huge house on the water because that spelled success for him. Even though he spends very little time enjoying the water, like boating, swimming or sailing, he chose to build a house there after comparing himself to his successful peers. If the Joneses have a big house on the water, then maybe he should too. Now Scott weighs his decisions against whether or not he will feel joy or fulfillment. This practice has him saying no to a lot more things, which has been both edgy and empowering.

It's helpful to write down the things you want. Then write down how it will feel when you get what you want. I want $1 million dollars so that

I'll feel secure about my future. It's the feeling we are chasing (secure), not the things ($1 million). When we compare ourselves, it's more powerful to hone in on the feeling we think they are experiencing and then figure out how we can experience it too in our own way.

What's Their Story

I feel like comparing is something we do without thinking about how close we are to reality. Going back to Facebook, when I see a family of four who is doing something amazing like hiking the Annapurna trail in Nepal, I automatically feel like a slug and a loser. When I meet people who I've secretly envied, I have learned that they often struggle too. No, it's not a big surprise, but it helps me to pull myself back from the comparison ledge when I can remind myself I have no idea what their story is.

I tend to use comparison as a way to put other people on a pedestal and put myself at a lower level. For instance, there is a woman who lives in my community who I see as a social and business powerhouse. She's a high-level executive, makes big deals happen, has a large family that appears close knit, and is incredibly attractive to boot. While we share many of the same interests, I have held myself back from connecting with her. That critical voice in my brain compares me to her and comes up painfully short. How could someone like her want to talk with someone like me? What could I possibly offer a person like her? Why would she even make time for someone like me? That voice mistreats me.

Having done loads of personal and professional development, I've been able to overcome many of my psychological barriers. I found the courage to invite her to coffee to discuss an idea of mine. Thankfully, she promptly agreed to meet. Over coffee, she shared with me how she was a stay at home mom for a long time, which really surprised me. I assumed that she had been slogging it in the corporate world this whole time getting knocked around, learning how to wheel and deal with bigwigs and building up her professional acumen. Suddenly, she became more human to me. What I had built up in my mind about how she got where she is was completely false. I was once again reminded that I usually don't know diddly about someone else and my assumptions are part of the problem.

I have two teenagers and I see comparison running rampant with them. They make up stories about their peers all the time. This friend has it so easy because her parents are rich and they bought her a car. That kid is so lucky because everyone likes him. She gets all A's because she's so smart. He gets all the girls because he's so cute. When I assure them that these other kids have their own issues, my children are not convinced. It's usually not until one of their peers shares a vulnerability with them that they realize that I may be right. Because they are teens, they gleefully remind me of the same thing when I compare myself to someone else.

Fairy Tale World

I found it troubling that we all use comparison even though it causes so many problems. I wanted to understand more, so I researched the reasons why we compare so often. The obvious reason is evolutionary as it allowed us to size up others for mates or enemies or tribe members. The more subtle reason lies in how our brains are wired. It turns out that when we make up a story in our mind about something, our brain gets a boost of serotonin as a reward regardless if the story is accurate. In other words, the brain cannot detect truth from falsity. We can believe that feelings are facts. That freaked me out that our brains just want the story and cares nothing about whether or not it's true. In other words, our stories, both true and false, make us feel good.

I had a client named Joe. He's in his 40's, married with a blended family and owns a retail store. His big challenge was his relationship with his wife. He wanted to feel more connected but also harbored years of resentments from past wrongs that she had committed against him. When we dissected the story he had made up in his head about her, it was heavy in the fairy tale category. He had made up a story about her having control over him and loving the power she lorded over him. In his mind, he was being victimized. He assumed that she enjoyed toying with him, like a cat with a mouse. He wondered if he should end the marriage and cut his losses.

When we challenged his stories, we came to find that there was very little evidence to prove that they were true. After only 3 months, he came to discover that she was suffering from childhood traumas that had her behaving in ways that caused her shame and guilt. He learned that she needed to have a safe space to share what she was feeling and not be judged by him. When he was able to meet her at that place, their relationship healed a bit. He erased the fairy tale stories in his mind with ones that were based in reality. They came to know each other better, which led to a deepening of their connection and intimacy.

It's so unfair that our brains reward us for something that keeps up from connecting with the people we love. Once we learn this, we can set about to deconstruct our stories and challenge their accuracy. I can't count how many times I hear people say, "When I learned more about this person, I saw them totally differently."

An Order of Comparison with a Side of Self Righteousness

If we know we are wired to compare and it's a big obstacle for most of us, then our next step is to minimize the detrimental effects. Not surprisingly, a good place to begin is to become aware of it. Then I like to throw in one of my favorite questions. How does comparing yourself to others serve you? When I once again lose my willpower and land on Facebook and fall into the doom loop of comparing myself, I can remind myself that this behavior is serving me in some fashion. Normally, it's procrastinating or boredom or distracting me from something I need to be focusing on.

I'm married to one of the nicest men on the planet. My husband is kind and patient and humble. When we first had children, our relationship went into a tailspin. Sleep deprivation coupled with the enormous responsibility of caring for another human 24/7 added pressure to an already tense situation. We were stressed out, exhausted and at our wits end most days. When I would start to feel overwhelmed, I desperately searched for a place to lay the blame. Since he was the other responsible party in the house, it was common for my finger to point directly at him. I would then use comparison as a sword to cut him down and bring him to my level of misery. In this way, I would prove that it was HIS fault that I felt incompetent and worthless. I did more diapering, feeding, clothing, bathing, cooing, and rocking than he did, therefore I was absolutely justified in my self-righteous anger towards him. It served me to blame him because then I didn't have to own my faults, mindsets and behaviors.

It might sound trite but we use comparison to make ourselves feel better. When I was at the gym the other day, a younger friend was admiring the strength of another woman doing pull ups. As we all admired this woman's strength and back muscles, my young friend said, "Well, she was a gymnast." This statement was loaded with comparison and smugness. This made her feel better. And it excused her from trying a pull up. There is a tempting benefit to comparison that, at times, we cannot forgo.

More _____ Than You

There are 7.4 billion people in the world. As a coach, I sometimes have to say things that make me uncomfortable. This is one of those moments. Here goes. There will always be someone richer, skinnier, prettier, smarter, younger, older, more educated, more experienced, more gregarious, etc. than you. This means comparison is a game you'll never win. When we get caught up in judging ourselves against what we perceive in others, the carrot will always be just out of reach. While we would never intentionally set ourselves up to fail, we still do it over and over and over again. Let's stop that, shall we?

During my engineering career, I constantly compared myself to my engineering peers who I believed to be smarter, faster, more creative and more polished than me. Every time I felt like I had crossed a threshold and caught up to them, I would find a different person with whom to compare myself. That was always the game. When I felt like I might be reaching the person I'd been chasing, I'd suddenly scan the horizon and find a different person to chase who was much farther ahead of me. This led to a constant state of inadequacy and not-good-enough-ness.

Again, we would never set ourselves up for failure, and yet trying to be as good as or more than anyone else never feels as good as we think it will. Then, to make matters worse, we keep moving the goal line on ourselves. My wise peer coach, Emma, who is in her 50's and has had a vast array of diverse life experiences once shared with me that she decided early into motherhood to become a good enough mother. The idea was a new one for me. What would it mean if I were good enough? Redundantly, is good enough good enough? I'd been led to believe that we should reward pushing and striving and sweating and struggling and gritting our teeth. When I considered what kind of mother I might be if I accepted the concept of good enough, I felt lighter, freer and relieved.

Stay Focused

A different benefit of comparing ourselves to others is that it is a wonderful distraction. For anyone that has a child, you know how a child will use comparison to distract you from the issue at hand.

"Did you clean your room?"

"Well, Susie didn't clean her room and I don't see you giving her a hard time!"

The purpose of comparison is to take the spotlight that is on one child and turn it on the other. Makes sense when others do it, but can we notice it when we do it to ourselves.

Melanie is a client in her mid 30's who runs her own boutique event planning business. She's new to the business owner gig, and she often finds herself frantically hustling to build her business justifying it by comparing herself to other businesses in the area. The pace of growth might feel good to her, but when she looks around and sees other businesses farther along than hers, she panics and tries to grow faster. This eventually leads to her feeling exhausted, and she is unfocused and forgetful about her original vision.

As we untangled the web of assumptions and comparisons that she had weaved together, we found that her business was just another representation of her proving herself. There were a series of if-then statements that she believed would lead to her salvation. Unfortunately, her need for unconditional love and validation, as a result of her upbringing, was popping up in her professional realm. She didn't want to feel unloved, not good enough and rejected. So she distracted herself by comparing herself to others and then busying herself by kicking up the pace. This only served to delay the day of reckoning, when from sheer exhaustion and frustration she would recognize she had gone completely off course. We would dissect these behaviors and then overlay them with her beautiful vision she has for her life and business. It was like a reset button that had her re-focus her efforts on what she truly wanted and put on blinders that kept out meaningless distractions, like comparison.

Most distractions come from our need to alleviate some kind of discomfort. When I'm bored, I distract myself with food. When I feel anxious, I distract myself with comparison. When I feel gloomy, I distract myself by binge watching Netflix. With food. It's always enlightening to bring some awareness to the ways that we distract ourselves and then dive deeper into what it is that has us wanting distraction.

I don't believe that comparison is all bad. Instead, I want to highlight the ways comparison can keep us from becoming better versions of ourselves. Many of the people in my life and in my coaching practice get caught up in comparison in ways that don't serve them well. We all know how to compare and it comes easily to us. What is difficult is extracting ourselves from comparisons that become barriers to our growth and development.

SELF REFLECTIONS

1. Is it serving you to focus on the other person rather than yourself?

2. What are the thoughts and words you're saying to yourself when you are in self judgment and comparison?

3. How often do you secretly wish you had what someone else has?

CHAPTER TEN.
OBSESSION WITH OUR IDEAS

Obsession is the wellspring of genius and madness.

MICHEL DE MONTAIGNE

W e may believe so deeply in our ideas that we become obsessed with them. We can see how our idea can be applied everywhere, like the Greek father with his bottle of Windex in *My Big Fat Greek Wedding* who said: "Any ailment from psoriasis to poison ivy could be cured by Windex." As we come up with solid solutions and innovative ideas, it's easy to plow forward and run over people in our path. We can convince ourselves that we are on the right track and all we need to do is implement something regardless of what others might say. We may even go so far as to point out successful characters from history who rammed ideas through naysayers and became heroes or winners or changed the world in some way. If we put on blinders, we miss out on opportunities to see even greater ideas. Applying conviction to our inherent intuition is the clear path to endless possibilities.

All Done

When I come up with a great idea, I am ready to implement, perform and realize it. I don't want to kick it around. I don't want to see if there are any flaws. I just want to go out and do it. It's easier to become obsessed with my idea than it is to consider alternatives. By continuing to focus on my idea, I don't have to slow down, open my mind and listen to anyone else. When I become obsessed with an idea, it's as though I see a myriad of possibilities where it can be applied. I can be on the implementation path, rather than the thinking, considering, planning path.

One of my clients, Mike, was obsessed with becoming a partner in his law firm. He had worked there for several years, and there was no shortage of ideas that Mike was chomping at the bit to implement. Time and time again, when Mike offered his ideas to the leadership team, he was rebuffed. Figuring that he didn't rank high enough, he started to focus on becoming partner so he could have a bigger say in the business. He worked more hours than everyone else. He took on work that no one else wanted. He volunteered to head up committees, manage teams and network for the firm. He was burning the candle at both ends, refusing to consider whether or not his idea of becoming partner was a good solution to getting the results he wanted. His spouse was mad at him, his kids felt less connected to him and he was exhausted.

When he and I started working together, we spent weeks just defining the problem. Mike discovered that his ideas were rebuffed for all sorts of reasons; the culture didn't want to take any risks, the leadership team was not looking to improve performance, and they couldn't agree on an IT approach. Mike had become obsessed with the idea that a partner position was the solution, the only solution. When we expanded his perspective by focusing on what energized Mike, challenged his underlying beliefs about being a partner as we explored other options to get what he wanted, he realized that he didn't really want to become a partner. Instead, he wanted to be able to fix the problems and work on the culture of the organization. By working hard and adding more and more responsibilities to his plate, he no longer found any joy in his work. Once we clarified what he actually wanted, he was able to let go of his singular drive to become a partner. Imagine carrying around an extra 50-pound sack and being able to put it down and leave it behind. This is how Mike felt when he shifted his focus.

Sometimes our ideas really are terrific, which makes it easy to want to apply them everywhere. We can see how our ideas could solve many issues. However, we have to also take into account reality. By keeping an open mind, seeking feedback and entertaining other possibilities, our ideas can be improved and are more likely to be implemented.

Coming On Too Strong

We can all think of a person who has really deeply held beliefs about something and how it can be off-putting for those around them. Sometimes big idea people can come off the same way. If we have already thought through all the different scenarios of how our ideas will make things better, then we take for granted the mental digestion process that people need when hearing something for the first time. Passion and emotion are great drivers for change, but they can also be met with resistance, especially if the passion for an idea is not shared. If we don't listen to others and are aggressive in our language or tone, we can then be seen as ramrodding our ideas down other's throats

For example, here are the steps to coming on too strong and not getting ideas understood, accepted and approved.

Step 1. Think outside the box.

Step 2. Come up with a great idea.

Step 3. Become obsessed with it because you like it so much.

Step 4. Consider how the idea can be applied everywhere.

Step 5. Be unwilling to take time to think the idea through and seek feedback.

Step 6. With blinders firmly in place, become securely attached to the idea.

With the process broken down into separate steps, we can see where we might be able to interrupt the flow and change direction. Steps 1 and 2 are wonderful, as they can leverage who you are and fill you with energy and enthusiasm. We get into trouble at Step 3 and beyond. In Step 3, instead of becoming obsessed, which closes the door to better options, we can seek out feedback from others. In Step 4, instead of considering how the idea can be applied everywhere, which is like jumping ahead before the idea has been vetted, we can try out the idea on a smaller scale first to see if it is viable. In Step 5, instead of plowing ahead, we can slow things down, think through different scenarios, and gather input from others. In Step 6, instead of becoming attached to our idea, we can acknowledge that there may be better ideas and consciously detach ourselves from the assumption that ours is the best one.

A colleague of mine, Nicole, has her own consulting business that specializes in leadership training. She has over 20 years of experience in the corporate world where she started to research the science and models behind personality assessments. The more she learned, the more she came to believe that personality assessments could be powerful tools to improve how leadership teams perform. She was both excited about the assessment she created and passionate about changing how people think about each other. When she approached a potential client, she would come off very strong. She spoke quickly with a lot of energy and was difficult to follow. Her passion was obvious, as was the resistance of the people listening to her. It's almost as though the stronger she pitched her assessment, the stronger the potential client would resist. After one pitch, a potential client looked at me and said, "Listening to her is like drinking from a fire hose."

Nicole's obsession with her model was so obvious to her. She couldn't imagine others not seeing her assessment in any way other than how she did. She was so focused on her own assessment that she would become emotional when people didn't choose her work. On one occasion, she sent an email stating how detrimental it would be to not use her work. If she wanted to make friends and influence people, she was flunking the basics. Her assessment may be truly transformational, but her obsession with it hindered people from wanting to try it.

When I was a consultant, I remember watching the older guys in my company offering really great ideas and watching how uncommitted they were to the client's answer. They would always preface their ideas by saying it's only one option, and there were always others. They were wholly unattached to whether or not the client saw the value in what we were proposing. With less passion and emotion on our side, the client seemed more open to giving our idea a try. By being less attached to the idea, the idea somehow becomes more attractive.

Running Out Of Steam

Imagine having a great idea that you are convinced is an absolute no brainer, presenting it to the powers that be and having it rejected. Is the idea not a good one? Was it the presentation? Was it clear how this idea would solve their problems? You dust yourself off, regroup and head off to your next presentation, only to be rebuffed again wondering why you can't make any headway. I think we all have a threshold of rejection before we admit defeat, so your great idea might languish on the vine because your obsession hinders your ability to see things more clearly. Einstein defines insanity as trying the same approach and expecting a different result. The big drawback is that it wears big idea people down. After meeting nothing but active resistance, they run out of steam.

I had a very powerful conversation with an executive director of a non-profit named Michelle. She is a true visionary who started up this non-profit over a decade ago. She had a big dream and came to realize it through this organization. During the growth and success of her non-profit, she continued to dream big and come up with unique and innovative ideas. She came to me because she felt like she'd hit a wall. She'd lost the confidence of her Board, her volunteers, and her employees. She was burning out and couldn't seem to see what was happening.

During our conversation, she detailed the issues she faced. When I asked her what she wanted, she gave the typical answers, like more staff, better Board members and having her employees do what she asks. So I asked her what would be better than that. When she looked stunned, I knew I had shifted her mindset. After a long silence, she responded that she wanted a true partner in the business who would be able to handle her out-of-the-box thinking and bring her ideas to life. She became very emotional, which tells me that she was getting close to the truth inside her heart.

To an outsider, it appeared that she had worn out her staff, volunteers, Board, and, most importantly, herself. By the time we met, nearly all of her ideas were rejected and she was met with resistance on a daily business.

Her plan before we met was to start hiring temporary staff to help get her caught up on her enormous workload. After we met, she realized that she wanted to find a high-level partner who could provide her with critical feedback on her big ideas and then be able to handle the detailed work of moving the ideas through the organization. Michelle saw this approach as being much more sustainable and exciting.

5 Things to Consider with Your New Idea

I have so many examples of being totally convinced that my idea was the right approach and not being able to implement it. Here are five questions to consider when implementing a new idea.

1. Is my idea the best one? This is where feedback is critical and brainstorming can lead to even better ideas. Henry Ford said, "If I asked people what they wanted, they would've told me faster horses." Faster horses were not the best idea. Instead, the motor car was.

2. Is it the right time for my idea? If you are a visionary, then it's always a good time to implement something new. However, determining how all the players involved will be impacted can sometimes allow a natural best time to surface. Sending a human to the moon happened at a really opportune time in American history and forever changed how we thought of ourselves and how others thought of us.

3. Do I really care enough to keep working on implementing my idea? If you never run out of ideas, then follow through may be a struggle for you. Before plowing forward with an idea, it can be helpful to step back and determine just how far you are willing to go to carry an idea through to

completion. When I was pregnant with my children, I was adamant that they would speak a foreign language. They are currently teens, and neither child sssssssspeaks a foreign language. I just didn't care enough about this great idea to make it happen.

4. Is my idea inherently flawed, out of the realm of reality or just met with resistance because the culture doesn't want innovation? Human flight was thought to be flawed and impossible when it was just a matter of persistence along with trial and error. By the time society felt like it might be a plausible idea for humans to fly, two brothers in North Carolina were already well on their way to getting and staying airborne.

5. Is the culture resistant to the change? If the culture will not support change, then the idea won't matter. Think of how long it took for societies to accept that the earth orbited the sun and our planet is indeed round and not flat. Both Copernicus and Galileo were shunned and threatened for exposing their ideas.

As I have watched friends, family, clients, and colleagues all burn out after becoming obsessed with an idea they thought was the right one for them, it seems to me that this obsession serves us in some way. Perhaps it means we don't have to swallow our pride or we have a perception that is not in alignment with reality. When we keep having the same challenge over and over again, it can be an indication to step back, re-assess and then change direction if appropriate. Finding a person who can challenge our ideas can have us remove the blinders and open up our mind which minimizes repetitive energy drains.

Can't See My Blind Spots

If you have kids, you can probably remember a time when they made a decision to do something that you could quickly see wouldn't work. They will continue to try to make the idea work, only to find that it just won't. As they try to force a solution that doesn't fit, they are unable to see how it will not work. When they are so occupied with implementing an idea, they are unable to see their own blind spots. My example is when my daughter was 18 months old and was putting farm animal magnets on the fridge. One by one, she would squat down to pick up a magnet off the floor and place it on the face of the fridge. At one point, she picked up a magnet and tried to place it on another magnet. When it didn't stick, she seemed a little surprised but picked it up and tried to stick it on top of the same magnet again. It dropped to the floor. After 3 more tries and failures, she looked at me and cried. She couldn't see that the magnet would only stick to the enormous magnetic surface of the fridge but not the non-magnetic surface of another magnet. Once I pointed this out to her, she stopped crying and continued sticking the remaining animals on the fridge. She was ready to accept the feedback, she could understand it and she could move forward successfully.

My client, Nate, owns an insurance company. He is entrepreneurial and has a different approach that he wants to bring to the world of insurance. He believes that the quicker he grows, the more successful he will be. So he has a strategy of networking, marketing and advertising like mad to get the word out and attract as many customers as possible. When we started working together, I got a sense that he always had one eye on everyone else, as though he feared falling behind the pack. His desire was to grow the business without losing himself along the way. He knew, intellectually, that he wasn't in a race, but his fear of what others thought of him was driving his behavior to hustle 24/7.

We explored what he wanted to do with his business, and we really dug into the dream he had for his company. When we addressed his obsession with growing quickly, he admitted he assumed that hustling, hurrying and being on the go all the time was how a business grows. I helped him to see his blind spot by asking him what would happen if he slowed down, and he replied he'd fall behind the pack. We discussed what the pack represented, how slowing down might improve his growth and how following his own internal compass was good enough. He came to realize that by giving his power to others, he was chasing his tail most days. Once he was able to take his power back, he settled in for a sustainable and steady growth trajectory that has resulted in him realizing the growth he wanted without having to hustle his way there.

Nate became really open to receiving feedback from the people in his life who had his best interests at heart. He didn't have to agree with the feedback, but he was open to hearing and considering it. He also found that when he knew his blind spots, he could reflect on decisions he was making and ensure that he was in the right mindset. His solutions improved. He served his clients more powerfully. He created truly unique products that set him apart from his competitors.

The top three blind spots that I see with my big thinking and visionary clients are with their assumptions related to money, what others think of them and control. I have a client, Jim, who has all the characteristics of leadership and advocacy, but he is stuck in his corporate job at a large financial firm. Because his big ideas are met with resistance inside his corporation, he wants to leave and start his own company. He has several business ideas, all of which excite and energize him, but he cannot make the break from the corporate paycheck and benefits. His spouse makes a good salary, they have a combined nest egg that is substantial and they live a relatively frugal lifestyle. To Jim, it seems obvious that he can't leave his corporate job to launch a new business. He takes it as a given that he will be poor, miss his mortgage payment and then live in a van down by the river. When challenged how long he could last if he had absolutely no paycheck, his answer was, "A few years." This answer actually surprised him. His blind spot that leaving the corporate world equals being broke has kept him stuck and dissatisfied for years. Once the blind spot was exposed, Jim was able to confirm its validity.

The second blind spot of fearing what others think of us is actually my blind spot. I wanted people to think I was smart, so I got an engineering degree. I wanted people to take me seriously, so I got an MBA and became the VP of a consulting firm. I wanted people to think I was funny, so I used humor to connect with people. It wasn't until I went against the status quo and alienated people that I was able to get over my fear of what others thought of me. By taking a stand for what I believed, I found a fellowship with others who felt the same way. Now, I have a career where my purpose is to serve and not please people, which means I have to face my fear of what my clients will think of me every day. I still have the fear, but now I don't let it control what I choose to do.

The third most common blind spot is that we cannot let go of control. Most of my clients have gotten to where they are by being in control of things, so asking them to shift control to others is a very difficult concept. I had a potential client, Will, who was the general manager of a large engineering company. His fear of letting go of control had him taking on all responsibility himself. He was working a crazy amount of hours, putting on a lot of weight, unable to sleep and felt totally overwhelmed and stressed. According to him, nobody in the organization could do things to his standard or he spent so much time telling them how to do what he wanted that it was quicker to just do it all himself. Will admitted that he liked being in control because then he knew things would be done the way he liked it. When I asked him to consider the costs of having to be in control, he sheepishly replied that it was costing him his overall health and wellness. When we discussed what was standing in his way to letting go of control, it turned out that he felt important and needed when he was so enmeshed in the organization. Will realized that he could find healthier ways to feel needed and wanted without diminishing his health and wellness.

We all have blind spots. When we become obsessed with our own ideas, we can act as though we have blinders on which only increases the span of our blind spots. Coming up with ways to take off the blinders is critical. Requesting and receiving feedback is edgy for most of us, but having someone who cares for us provide us with the truth is a gift. It helps us to see ourselves in a whole new way. Our ideas get better, and so do we.

SELF REFLECTIONS

1. How can you deliberately slow down the idea to completion process?

2. What kind of supports can you create so your ideas can be carried out?

3. Who can help you discover your blindspots?

CHAPTER ELEVEN

IDEAS GET ME HIGH

*"If you change the way you look at things,
the things you look at change."*

WAYNE DYER

I f you are someone who doesn't think like everyone else in the room, then you might find that new and innovative ideas energize you. When you hear about Elon Musk tackling the transportation problem in America, or you meet a group of engineers creating portable energy for rural areas in Africa, or you can get functional skin created by a 3D printer, you enter into a world of possibility which pumps you up. In short, ideas get you high.

Killer Buzz

One of the things that new ideas can do for me is provide me with a type of escape. I can complain and moan about the state of affairs, or I can think about how I wish things could be. Then I can pile more ideas on top of those ideas creating a buzz of ideas that get me high and have me hoping for the day when all my dreams come true. To me, this feels like a position of power because it's the opposite of the victim mentality.

When I feel helpless, generating ideas lifts my spirits and I feel a buzz of energy. When I'm at the airport and standing in the ticket line, security line, food line or boarding line, it's easy to become frustrated at the way air travel is being handled. If I can shift to all the things I would do if I could be ruler for a day, then I am having fun and being creative.

Jim, one of my clients, is working with me to plan his transition from his high level executive career to going out on his own. He is absolutely passionate about media and has really amazing ideas for resurrecting older forms of media in new and creative ways. During one of our sessions, Jim wanted to discuss how to start small with low risk. He had an idea that he wanted to explore, so we threw it on the table and batted it around. He had one idea that was simple, low risk and also had a low probability of getting him started in any appreciable way. After he proudly described his plan to me, I didn't say anything, waiting for more. After an awkward interlude of silence, he said, "That's it." So I answered, "What else?" Another long period of silence ensued.

Once Jim was tasked with coming up with other options, he had to shift his mindset from safe and low risk to more risky options. It's like I gave him permission to wade a little farther into the deep end. When he did, he came up with 10 other ideas for moving forward. Each new idea sparked more new ideas, and Jim was on a roll. I don't think I spoke for 15 minutes while Jim tossed new ideas out like a pitching machine. Here's the really fun part, Jim was alive. He was chock full of energy and possibility. When his fears popped up and he ventured back to the shallow end, I would gently redirect him to the deeper end. Jim was totally invigorated and left that session with a new-found purpose.

Eric, another client, is in the process of growing his lifestyle business. When we started working together, he was unsure about how to expand and didn't have the self-worth and confidence to talk to bigger players in the industry. He was playing small, but he knew he was capable of playing a bigger game. In one of our recent sessions, he wanted to walk away with a clear direction of where to grow the business. He had a low-risk series of steps, like adding some new discounts to his offerings, sprucing up his website and looking into new certifications. I couldn't wait to elevate his vision and pull the greatness out of him. In Eric, I saw someone who was transforming people's lives and whose work was so important and impactful that it should be integrated into every hospital and school in the country. When he shared that his goal of reaching 1,000 people, I asked him what if he changed that goal to 1 million people. Silence.

To answer the question, Eric had to shift over to a different part of his brain, like railroad tracks changing. Once he engaged the idea generator part of his mind, he became unstoppable. Every idea he threw out, I acknowledged him and then asked, "What else?" It was delightful to watch Eric come up with idea after idea and witness his energy levels rise. He was completely thrilled by the end of the session and had a list of actionable items that would up-level and grow his business.

Shift Perception

One of the things that a new idea can do is challenge deeply held beliefs and assumptions. For example, consider self-driving cars. I have an assumption that when my kids need a ride, I have to spend my time driving them. When I need to visit family for the holidays, I need to spend my time and attention on driving the two days it takes to get there. If I didn't have to drive, what would that mean? My perception is shifted and the possibility gates are wide open. The idea can generate the shift. Likewise, the shift can generate the idea. For example, when I asked my client to shift his goal from 1,000 to one million people, the new ideas rapidly burst out of him. As Tony Robbins says, "Successful people ask better questions, and as a result, they get better answers."

Another client, Wendy, has a deeply held belief that her current HVAC business cannot fulfill her. She hired me to partner with her to determine her purpose in the world. Her expectation is that her current business is in no way linked to her purpose. During a session, we explored what made Wendy feel alive. When she responded with all the things she had done in her life that filled her with energy and purpose, I wrote down the words that she used. I had a list of a dozen things. To shift her thinking from finding a new business out there somewhere to a current business that is right in front of her, I asked her how she could incorporate these dozen things into her HVAC business. She stalled and directed an expletive at me. Her brain was changing tracks. Click. After generating all sorts of new ideas for her current business, she sat back in her chair, crossed her arms over her chest and said, "This is good." Indeed.

There are so many times in my own life when a shift in perception allowed a new idea to break free, and when a new idea caused a shift in my perception. It's a chicken and egg phenomenon. If you are an out-of-the-box thinker, your big, bold ideas have the power to shift perceptions, and your different perspectives have the power to initiate big, bold ideas. Whether you begin with the idea or the shift, my hope is that you begin.

Accountability vs. Vision

Accountability is helpful when trying to reach goals. There's something about having to answer to someone else that drives us to complete the things we say we'll do. It's common for people to seek out life coaches for accountability to keep them on track, be better and do more. There is a distinction that I'd like to point out. If the vision isn't big enough, then accountability plays a major role. If the vision is big and bold and inspiring, then accountability will play a small role. My job as a coach is to elevate someone's vision until it is so big and juicy that nothing will get in their way.

I was having a session with my coach, Rich Litvin, and he was challenging me about defining my target market. I hemmed and hawed and said I wasn't sure. "I'm getting close and it'll become clear to me soon," I rambled. He shared with me that another client of his says he coaches the smartest people in the room. "Who do you coach, Allison?" I responded very matter of factly that I coach the person in the room who doesn't think like everyone else and finds themselves saying, "It doesn't have to be that way." Rich replied that'd be a great title for a book, and then asked if I wrote that book what the chapters might be. Then he asked if I could have anyone in the world write a foreword for me, who would it be. Duh, Oprah!

After our call, the idea of writing a book was bouncing around in my mind and I couldn't quite shake it. A half hour after our call, Rich posted a fake book cover with my title, my name and a quote from Oprah in our closed Facebook group. Once I saw it, I wanted it so badly. It was too delicious and juicy to pass up. This very book is the result of Rich elevating the vision with me. I will finish writing the book in 4 months, and I never needed someone to hold me accountable.

When I have initial coaching conversations with potential clients, I love to listen to the thing they want and then get curious about why they want it. Then I take their want and ask them what it'd be like if they could achieve it on a scale so much bigger than they ever imagined. For example, I was coaching an executive in a large housing business. He shared lots of pain points of his current position and said he was seeking coaching to overcome them. I told him that his vision of our work together was boring. I asked him to tell me more. Then I asked him to tell me what he'd do if he were ruler for a day. His energy went up and he sat taller when he shared he really wanted the organization to treat their employees better. So I blew his want out of the water and asked what if his organization became a place where turnover was non-existent, where employees loved coming to work and evangelized about it, and where each employee was given the opportunity to make their own dreams a reality. Tick-tock and CLICK. His brain was shifting tracks. He sat back in his chair, looked at the ceiling and smiled. He responded that it would be super. Once he saw the elevated vision, he couldn't undo it.

Our own assumptions can really get in our way when we are trying to solve problems, live a wholehearted life, and find purpose and meaning in our work. We can quickly shift from being empowered to being a victim. We may want something with all our heart and soul, but we may not be able to do it alone. It can be a game changer to surround yourself with people who will magnify and amplify your visions, support you through the process, and challenge you to shift your mindset on a regular basis. When I saw the fake book cover that Rich created for me, I hired a book coach the next day! I don't know how to write a book. Heck, I barely know how to write. I am an engineer, remember? My book coach believes in me more that I believe in myself. Without her, this book would just be a thing that I want, rather than a dream I am realizing.

One More-itis

If you are an out-of-the-box thinker who never runs out of ideas, then you know there is a dark side. Your list of to-dos can become long and exhausting since it's difficult to know when to stop. This is where visionaries get stuck. For example, I want to create a course for the local university, create a leadership program for teens, coach amazing clients, create a coaching event and write a book. Oh yeah, I also want to change public education, raise wonderful children, cultivate a great marriage and train for a 50K with my best friend. Oy! When you think in big ideas, you can easily drift into the land of overwhelm which is where we can suffer from one more-itis. This is where we can always do one more thing. Just like the fat man in the restaurant in the Monty Python skit, just one more wafer after a gargantuan meal caused him to literally explode.

My friend, Dian, is a huge dreamer. She is a social rebel with big, bold ideas. Because she is so passionate about the needs of her community, she has launched several initiatives. Any one initiative would be a lot for a person to manage, and Dian has many of these to corral. She rises early in the morning and goes to bed late in the evening. She lives on caffeine and she doesn't have time to take care of herself. She makes promises that she struggles to keep. She is late most of the time. For Dian, there is *always* one more thing she can do. While her heart is in the right place, she can be perceived as disorganized, flaky and irresponsible. This is the dark side of being a big thinker. Without supports in place to keep Dian on track, she runs off into the bottomless ditch endlessly.

Even with supports in place, we can run ourselves ragged. I have several coaches, a support group, a wonderful group of friends and family, and I still overextend myself. It's all for naught if we don't commit to taking care of ourselves. We have the best of intentions to eat well, exercise regularly, and sleep 8 hours each night. No support in the world can help you if you can't resist the temptation to take on one more thing. When I have overloaded my plate, I find that being present is a great way to snap me back to reality. Taking a deep breath, closing my eyes and experiencing the present moment brings me away from becoming obsessed with the past or the future and gently places me in the here and now. We have to do a lot of things well in order to be at our best, and a good start is to remember to be present and surround yourself with remarkable people.

For those of us business folks who can always do one more thing, we need to build a team with people. If we pair ourselves with people, like an assistant, who can break down our big ideas and do the busy work, then we won't get bogged down in the one more-itis. For us, busy work suppresses our ability to generate big ideas. When we can unload our ideas to someone who can break them down into bite sized pieces, then our busy minds can move forward. Because we all have a limited bandwidth, a support team can also keep us focused on 2 or 3 priorities at a time.

Beautiful Distraction

There's another dark side to being a big thinker with bold ideas. When I am uncomfortable in any way, I can leave the discomfort and hang out in the world of possibilities and rainbows. When the reality of a situation is staring me in the face, I can turn away and think about how it could be. I never run out of ideas. It's a gift and a curse. I can use my great ideas to create change or I can use them to distract me from my own discomfort (or both). What's so bad about not wanting to be uncomfortable? I believe my discomfort is trying to tell me something. I don't want to be uncomfortable, but the only way to get out of it is to acknowledge it. In other words, turn towards it rather than away from it.

I have a fear of what others think of me, and one way I deal with this fear is to charge a fee that I think a person will find reasonable rather than a fee that represents the value I bring. I have implemented some big, bold ideas in my coaching where, in addition to bringing my clients on an intellectual journey, I also bring them on physical journeys. These experiential field trips, as I call them, offer clients a new and powerful way to experience insights and growth. Yet, my fee is still the same. This makes me uncomfortable. So I want to turn away from it. What I realized is that I need to face my fears repeatedly in order to grow and build confidence. The insight that came forward was that I need to double my fees for one month. This ignites my fear, so I know I must be on the right path because my fear eventually changes into fearlessness. I'm then able to be more straightforward, hence, more productive with my clients. And myself.

One of my former clients, Karen, really wanted to embed professional development into her advertising business. Karen is a self-help junkie, and she loves to consider new and innovative ways to transform the people in her organization. During our time together, she would launch these terrific initiatives sometimes in an effort to avoid the discomfort of what she needed to do. At times, Karen could face her discomfort and really hit a home run. Other times, she couldn't bring herself to do it. Karen is human, and she gets to be imperfect and flawed like the rest of us. When our contract was up, Karen elected not to continue working with me. I still check in on her to see how she's doing. Unfortunately, her business is not doing well. She has slipped back into her old pattern of refusing to relinquish total control and owning all authority. She is still launching new initiatives and dreaming big, but none of the initiatives are addressing her own stumbling blocks.

Humans are an amazing and sometimes predictable lot. We avoid pain, which makes sense and is logical. However, not all pain is bad for us. A pushup can cause pain, but it also builds strength. Making amends to someone we have wronged can be a painful experience, but it also relieves us from long term suffering. Even a vaccination hurts when it's administered, but it prevents the agony of some debilitating or potentially fatal illness. The dark side of being a big thinker is that it can lead us to distract ourselves from things that may need our attention. Humans are designed to avoid discomfort. Creating a life where we have the ability to face our pains, be they emotional or physical, can pay big dividends to ourselves and the people around us.

SELF REFLECTIONS

1. How can you intentionally shift your own perception on an issue that is bothering you?

2. What is something you would love to create? How can you upgrade that vision into something that has you salivating?

3. How are you using ideas to avoid an issue you'd like to overcome?

CHAPTER TWELVE.
SAY NO

"Saying no does not always show a lack of generosity and that saying yes is not always virtue."

PAULO COEHLO

I t's not possible to do everything, but boy we sure try hard to squeeze it all in. If you are like me, then you say yes for all sorts of reasons that continue to add obligations to your already full plate. And if you're a big ideas person who thinks differently, then you probably have plenty of initiatives you'd like to see come to culmination. Ideas give us energy. They give us possibility-gasms™. They tickle our hope. How can you say no to that? As a compulsive yes-ophile, I get it. Saying no is like fingernails on a chalkboard for me, but it can be one of the most powerful ways we can be at our best and do more good in the world.

Illusion of Control

Having control over anything other than ourselves is an illusion and it comes at a cost. It decreases creativity, lowers our ability to think outside of the box and has us behaving in a way that doesn't serve our highest good. There is this illusion that we can do everything, and it's sold to us by advertisers, employers and timeshare salesmen. The reality is that there is only one of us. The reality is that we cannot multitask. The reality is that there are only 24 hours in a day. Yes, you can do a lot. Sure, you can say yes most of the time. But think what your life might be like if you only focused on one or two projects that truly feed your soul. You are likely to experience more success, more progress, and more momentum.

There are some great case studies in MBA programs showcasing how the illusion of control can ruin a business. Just look at Uber and how it seems to sabotage its own successes with rampant lawsuits and bad behavior. The CEO seems to lack any moral compass and is caught time and time trying to shortcut major issues. He fought going public, listening to his lawyers and following the law in certain circumstances, which all seemed like ways to resist giving up control. He even referred to Uber as his wife. In the end, the CEO was forced to leave, which is the ultimate slap in the face for someone who prided himself on the being a lone wolf leader.

I don't mean to insinuate that you resist relinquishing control because you are an ego maniac or an immoral executive. Instead, we can all reflect on how we can learn to let go of the illusion of control. We can examine ways of handing over the baton. We can be intentional and strategic in the people to whom we give authority. If you have big, bold ideas and want to launch them, then create a team that empowers you. Just like a professional athlete, your team can include teammates, mentors, and coaches who challenge you, support you and make you better.

I Can Do It Myself

I have a friend who lost her husband suddenly. Many of her friends and acquaintances rallied around her, supporting her through the long and painful process of grieving for all the lost dreams and hopes that were buried with him. I marveled at her ability to accept the help and allow others to love and care for her. Almost a year after his death, she had surgery on her shoulder and she resurrected her support team to set up all the help she'd need. Instead of saying no, I can manage everything myself, I don't want to put you out or you'll probably resent having to bring me a meal or drive me somewhere, she went the opposite direction and put her needs out into the world. When she did, she found a small army of people only too happy to give her hand. She's a beautiful example of saying no to saying no.

I say yes really quickly for lots of the wrong reasons. I want people to like me. I want to feel needed. I want to be involved in something that I think is good and noble. I have to restrain my codependency and people pleasing tendencies when people make requests of me. Why? I will fill my days with yeses only to find that I didn't take care of the things that are most important to me, like my family, my friends and myself. God forbid I should allow someone to do something without my help. I mean, how would they manage? Sometimes I feel like if a God complex and people pleaser syndrome got together and had a baby that it'd be me.

Fact: We cannot do everything. Fact: There are only 24 hours in a day. Fact: If you can't take care of your own basic needs, like sleeping and eating, then you are no good to anyone else. When I am faced with a request, I try to weigh it against the things that might not happen if I say yes. Think sustainable.

Insulation Means Saying No

We may say yes for honorable reasons, but it can lead to distracting us from our important work. One way of insulating ourselves from things that pull us away from our meaningful work is to decline anything that doesn't bring you closer to that work. If you are a big thinker with a big heart, then you probably already have plenty of visions for better ways of doing things. Anything that delays you from realizing your big, bold dreams is to be avoided at all costs. Our world needs you to stay focused.

I can get myself all worked up over a great idea that I'll be saying yes before anyone even asks me for something. You had me at, "I got an idea." Recently, I had been asked to gather a team of up to 4 people and bring them to Liberia for a Leadership program. The possibilities of what this trip represented in my mind were endless and wonderful and transformational. How could I not go? When I floated the idea to my family, my husband and two children suddenly found themselves very interested in pushing the food around on their plates. "Well, what do you think?" My daughter bravely asked how I would have time to squeeze in this trip with everything else I had going on, like building a coaching practice, writing a book, being the President of the school board and starting up a leadership program for middle school kids. My son agreed and added that Liberia had an Ebola outbreak not too long ago. My husband seemed almost sad that I would even consider leaving the family for two weeks for yet another idea that had me moving farther from our family rather than closer to it. What's worse than saying no? Having to go back and say no after already saying yes, which is what I had to do. It was a good reminder to stay focused on the important work I'm already doing.

Recruit Teammates

One way that I have discovered I can still say yes to wonderful ideas is to recruit teammates. Because I can see the value in most ideas, it's a lot more fun to find a way to say yes, like finding other likeminded people who can be involved and provide value. Instead of having to say no, I can say I know someone who might be able to say yes.

Our local university has a continuing education department. They are always looking for new ideas, which is like an intellectual playground for someone who never runs out of ideas. Every time I meet with the continuing education team, I talk like a 6-year-old girl being asked what she wants for Christmas. How about a class on coaching? What about teaching people about overcoming people problems? I know, what do you think about bringing coaching cultures into local organizations? And don't even get me started on the leadership series we could create together. Alas, I agreed to create a curriculum and teach a 6-week course on coaching to business folks. I love the idea. I do not, however, love to write curriculum nor teach the content. But I said yes, so I can either back out, do it anyways or recruit some help. Thankfully, I met another life coach who was really interested in the course we are creating. After a few coffees, she wholeheartedly agreed to work on this course with me and is entertaining the idea of taking over for me after our pilot run. It's the best of both worlds.

If we can be creative, then we can find different ways to say yes to ideas that excite us. The beauty of creating a team is that they can commit to things whilst you move on to the next big idea. In fact, big idea people seem to be most effective when they partner with detail lovers. Big idea people can dream big, and detail people can get it done. Building a team is helpful, and creating a complimentary group of people is even better.

Matchmaker

Along the same lines of recruiting teammates is matching "idea people" with those who can help. There is no shortage of great ideas in the world.

If you are an outside of the box thinker, then you have an innate ability to find value in ideas that others miss. Because of this, you can catch an idea with merit and help elevate it. Then you may be able to rally the right people to carry the idea forward. Please note that you may not be the right people.

Just like a traditional matchmaker can see the values in two people and bring them together for the purposes of creating a lasting relationship, the community of out-of-the-box thinkers can see the values in big ideas and pair them with the folks that can assist in shouldering the load. The first step in my client enrollment process begins with a conversation, typically over a cup of coffee. I have met with hundreds of people, most of whom don't become my client. But I can serve them by putting them in touch with people who would be a good match for their needs. I've helped the university find a keynote speaker for the college of education. I've connected a local non-profit with a colleague in a different state so they can expand their programming across the country. I've asked professional chefs to work with a small organic baby food startup to scale the one person operation. If you get excited by new ideas and can see the value in them, then you can be a great idea people connector.

Matchmaking has allowed me to say no to being involved myself but saying yes to serving people in other ways. Like I said, I hate to say no. I can always find a way to help because I suffer from being a codependent, people pleaser who wants others to like me. It's been a relief for me to say no while simultaneously supporting others with names of people and organizations that may be right for them. So many people are looking for resources, so you can become a resource center.

Say What You Mean, Mean What You Say

Someone proposes an amazing idea. You are hooked. You see the potential, the value, the possibility. Your energy goes up. You start talking faster. You throw out ways to make the dream a reality. You think through all the people you know who can be involved. You are in! Then you wake up the next day and realize you already have too much going on and feel guilty for saying yes to something that you cannot commit to 100%. Maybe you stay the course and give less than 100%. Perhaps you back out and apologize. Either way, you are out of integrity. The moral of the story: be impeccable in your commitments

Because people who think differently are big idea types, there isn't an issue that they can't bat around like a cat with a toy to find multiple solutions and approaches. Our tendency is to say yes instead of no. This can result in being overwhelmed, not taking care of ourselves and residual feelings of guilt and resentment. When weighing our commitment to the next amazing idea, we can consider this single question. Can I commit 100%? If the answer is no, then we can take some time to decide what we can commit 100% to. For instance, I may not be able to commit to my friend's charity for human trafficking, but I can connect her with likeminded people who may want to get involved, or I can make a donation to her program, or I can ask some teachers if they'd consider having her come and educate our kids on the subject. There are lots of issues that resonate with me, but I cannot commit to all of them. If I can't give 100%, then I can prevent that yes from escaping my mouth and go to plan B.

I had a client, Bill, who ran a small accounting business. He was a big thinker and loved to talk about big ideas. He had difficulty staying on task and his team frequently commented on his tangential nature during weekly meetings. He had a tendency to say yes to most things, and his team became increasingly frustrated. He began the year by charging his team with significant growth targets. They agreed, but Bill was constantly distracted by other ideas. He said yes to ideas which took up more of his time and energy. He became a less effective leader and he was losing the confidence of his team. He was not being impeccable in his commitments, and it had a net negative effect.

During a weekly meeting with the team, he threw yet another big idea at the team and shared why he felt so energized by it. When he was finished, he was met with silence. So he asked his team what they thought. They responded that they didn't feel they could keep chasing the aggressive growth goals and take on new initiatives that seemed like distractions from those goals. Bill could see how the new initiatives would promote the goals, but his team could not. Bill was overcommitting, which resulted in him under-delivering to his team's needs. Thankfully, Bill was the type of guy who valued feedback and he was able to scale back and commit himself to focusing on his team. Of course, when we talk, he still has those big ideas ruminating in his mind, but now he weighs them against his own capacity to commit fully.

Deep Inner Work

We say yes to things for lots of reasons, many of which have nothing to do with being excited about the thing we are saying yes to. I might say yes to driving my mom to her doctor appointment because I don't want to feel guilty. I might say yes to taking my kids shopping because I want them to love me and think I'm cool. I might say yes to being on a committee because I think it will raise my social status in the community. Notice how my yeses have nothing to do with the thing I'm agreeing to do. When my yeses are accompanied with an ulterior motive, then I probably need to dig deeper into my intentions.

In my experience, people who have the highest level of peace and joy are the ones who know who they are. They have done the deep work of figuring out why they are on this earth. How do they know? The answer I get is self-awareness. I think this means that they have spent time and energy discovering who they are in this world. They realize that it's the only way to find a path forward without internal conflicts and feelings of guilt and resentment. They have high integrity because they know who they are. They say no to things because they know who they are. They don't let their egos and critical voices run their lives because, you guessed it, they know who they are. The deep inner work of self-awareness is hugely beneficial.

In my coaching mastermind group, I find myself feeling small and insignificant. Of course, this is all me and my not good enough fears. During one of our sessions, one of the coaches said something really confrontational to another coach. I was so uncomfortable with the tension that I wanted to hide under a table. But I stayed and watched the reactions of both coaches, like studying primates in a zoo. After the ordeal, I asked the coach how she finds the courage to say things that are edgy, uncomfortable and provocative. She looked at me and replied she spends a lot of time and energy on deep inner work to know herself.

How does one go about knowing themselves better? I think I may have discovered one path that is working for me and my clients. Anytime I have a struggle, I look for the fear. Then I figure out how to face the fear as my tendency is to distract myself from it with being busy, eating crap and binge-watching Netflix. When I focus on the fear, there is a place I have to go that is incredibly uncomfortable. It's the dirty diaper analogy where I figuratively force myself to sit in a dirty diaper and not change it. By sitting in it, I can notice the thoughts and feelings that arise. I don't judge them, just notice them. When I'm doing this, my brain gets wonky and keeps offering me ways to escape, but I choose to sit in it anyway. Here's something really helpful that I've learned. The discomfort will end. It doesn't last forever. This single fact has been very helpful as I head into a dirty diaper sitting. When I know that the discomfort will end, I can allow it to be.

When we decided to pull our daughter out of traditional school and enroll her in an online program, I went to a deep, dark place. I was filled with worry and dread. My critical voice was so loud, and it was most intense when I went to sleep at night and when I awoke in the morning. My fear was on high alert, and I was on the carousel in crazy town cycling through all the catastrophes that would occur. I worried that she would never learn to make friends, become isolated and depressed, and live in our basement as an adult. I wondered if I was a bad mother, if we were running from our problems, and if we were enabling her. Each night before bed, I would get this discomfort in the pit of my stomach and my mind would race. Instead of judging it, I decided to notice it. I would always fall asleep but I would awaken in the middle of the night and early in the morning with the same discomfort and racing thoughts. I was really uncomfortable.

The good news is that the discomfort slowly dissolved like an Alka-Seltzer tab. At first, when the tablet is dropped into the glass, the water begins to bubble. Then the fizzing starts and the water becomes chaotic and opaque. After a while, the water is clear, the tab has dissolved and the glass is calm. There wasn't a moment of clarity when my discomfort cleared. Instead, each day the discomfort was less than the day before. Weeks later, there are still twinges and pops of discomfort but nothing like the intensity of what I went through those first few days.

To what end you ask. Well, I am delighted to tell you that I am now resolute in my parenting skills. I learned that all my fears about my daughter were mostly false. I'm more confident in my mothering than ever before because I know who I am as a mother. I don't parent like anyone else because I'm me. I know that I can listen to my daughter and find a way to get her needs met. I can let go of the need to have her be like other kids, or more importantly what I perceive to be like other kids. I am no longer embarrassed about my daughter being home-schooled because I am sure that it's what is right for her right now. On the other side of fear is relief, peace, and confidence.

Here's how I envision the fear process, which I have titled the Alka-Seltzer Model of Self-Awareness.

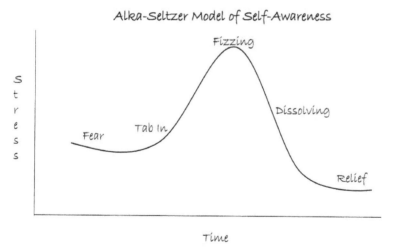

In the beginning, denying the fear has our stress sitting at a tolerable level. When we choose to face the fear, our stress goes up and stays up for a period of time. At some point, the stress begins to dissipate and decrease, eventually landing at a level much lower than where it began. This is the payoff.

In order to say no to things, it sure helps to know who you are which can involve facing your fears. I've witnessed my family members, clients, and even myself face our fears, sit in the discomfort and come out the other side knowing who we are and what we need to do. It's hard to convince ourselves to go to that place of discomfort. After all, who would willingly accept pain when there are some many delicious distractions out there? The answer is that the heavy weight of fear and worry can be lifted. It comes at a cost, but one that is worth paying in my opinion.

SELF REFLECTIONS

1. When you say yes, what is the real reason?

2. How does it feel when you say yes to something that you don't want to do?

3. How can you say no without guilt?

CHAPTER THIRTEEN

STAY PRESENT TO AVOID THE FUTURIZING IMPULSE

If you are depressed, you live in the past. If you are anxious, you live in the future. But, if you are at peace, you live in the present.

Lao Tzu

For those of us who love to play with possibilities and think of all the iterations of wonderfulness that can occur from great ideas and initiatives, we have a tendency to fly off into la-la land like a helium balloon released into the atmosphere. Possibility-gasm™, weee! We can stay lost in the ether, which is fun and exciting and energizing but it can also be impractical and ineffective. Instead, we have to come back to earth and play in the moment, because being present can serve us in so many ways.

Idea Ball

Betty, one of my colleagues, is a big idea thinker. She is always raising the bar on ideas, thinking about bigger and better possibilities and she tends to wear some people down. I was listening to some folks lamenting about Betty's compulsive idea generation, and they likened her ideas to beach balls at a concert. She would lob an idea (AKA beach ball), and then the idea would get bumped again and again never touching the ground but instead bouncing around in the air. People tended to roll their eyes at Betty's ideas. Even though some her ideas were great, her unfocused and disorganized approach lacked traction. Just like at the end of a concert, Betty's ideas would lay motionless on the ground, left behind with nowhere to go and no one to take them on.

It seems that having the ability to dream up new ideas also needs a system to build a strategy and plan around them. Just bouncing from idea to idea isn't terribly helpful. For example, there are programs in schools and universities where businesses send a problem to students to solve in new and innovative ways. The kids get to think about all the options, throwing all their ideas on the table and dreaming big. The business receives the ideas for consideration and then does the strategic planning around the ones that are plausible for their organization. This process is effective and exploits the strengths of each group. Students are not typically concerned with all the minutia required to promote an idea and push it through an organization. Businesses know the process of creating systems around ideas but aren't always strong at thinking outside of the box. Win-win.

If you are an idea creator who loves lobbing new ideas into the crowd, then you may want to consider finding a strategic thinker to pick up your idea and make it a reality. If you are really brave, you can toss your ideas to a person who isn't fond of new ideas. For instance, I used to work with a colleague whose first answer was always no. Part of him loved to argue and the other part didn't like to consider new ways of doing things. By having to defend my great ideas to this idea blocker, I was forced to find multiple ways to defend my ideas. The result was that my ideas had a finer filter, which yielded more reasonable options.

What-iffing

There are two kinds of what ifs. One is what if bad thing happens. The other is what if an even better thing happens. People who think outside of the box can get caught up in the second kind of what-iffing. Picture this. You are in a board room. Someone presents an idea. You like the idea and state as much verbally. Then you build on the idea, tossing out what if scenarios at a rapid pace. You're floating away from the group and are now lost somewhere between the troposphere and stratosphere. C'mon back, you. This is the type of what-iffing that can get many of us ignored, scoffed at or just plain shot down.

Let's use an example from my personal life. Our daughter suffers from anxiety and depression. As a young teen, she goes through periods of great difficulty. In order to help her find ways to build her self-esteem and confidence, we've discovered her gift for understanding animals. She has a dog, a cat and 5 guinea pigs. She volunteers at the local humane society. She is the go-to person in our neighborhood for pet sitting. After completing horse therapy with her therapist, she started taking horseback riding lessons. I shared with my husband how wonderful she did with her first riding lesson and then began "what-iffing" all over him. I started with -- what if I took lessons with her and we learned to care for and ride horses without an instructor. We could lease a horse or buy a horse and get some land in the country. We could even build a barn... Off I drifted, blabbering about running a farm/school for girls with anxiety and depression while my husband looked at the unwashed piles of laundry on the floor and dirty dishes that we couldn't keep up with.

This isn't to say that elevating visions is a bad idea. It's just that for some of us who love to run off on tangents of what ifs and possibility-gasms can build some awareness of our tendencies. It's wonderful to have big dreams. If I want to build a farm school for anxious girls someday, then I can keep that beautiful vision in my mind as I make day to day decisions. I can also be cognizant of our family's immediate needs and do my best to stay present and live in reality. And do some laundry once in a while. Living in the future can be a distraction, so coming back to earth and being in the moment is a good skill to hone.

Accepting Reality

When we start to consider what could be, we can easily become infatuated with a utopia that doesn't and cannot exist. Think about the issues that our culture argues about: taxes, free trade, net neutrality, common core standards, standing for the national anthem, immigration. These are complex issues with lots of moving parts. We might wish, imagine, fantasize about a world where these issues are easy to solve, but if that were the case then they'd probably be solved already. When we get frustrated at the pace or the rejection of new ideas, we can remind ourselves to take a big dose of reality.

When our daughter was hospitalized for depression, I suffered greatly. I frantically searched for the thing(s) to blame for her illness. It's those darn cell phones and social media and our immediate gratification culture and public education and the economy and I grabbed her really hard when she was two years old out of frustration. As I sat in my sadness and fear, I wondered how we could get her back to "normal". How could we help her to clear out the distorted thoughts that swirled around in her mind? How could we keep her from going in the deep, dark hole next time? How could we cure her, control her, fix her? Then I got a big dose of reality from my coach. She said, "Allison, she will never be normal." It felt like a sucker punch to the solar plexus. The reality is that she'll always have distorted thinking. She will always suffer from depression. She will never be cured. Gulp. That reality is a large, dry, bitter pill to swallow. The sooner I choke it down, the sooner I can get on with coming up with better ideas.

Regardless of the issue, it's an effective strategy to stand back, look around and ask yourself, "What is the reality here?" There is a saying that suffering is caused by our mind's refusal to accept reality. By accepting what is, you can get on with life. The resentments, blaming, and shoulding can stop. If my daughter is never going to live a normal life, then I better get on board and adjust my expectations. Once I've accepted reality, I can come up with ideas that are more harmonious and useful for the situation at hand.

Futurizing Prevents Being Present

Soaring above everyone in the room in my possibility bubble can be a really helpful way to sidetrack myself. I have noticed that I can use futurizing, which is the act of thinking about the future, to keep me from being present. When discomfort arises, the emotional kind, I love to jump right into the future and think about all the things that will be better out there in the future. Futurizing can be the same as eating Nutella out of the jar with a spoon; it feels good in the moment. By being an outside the box thinker, I am really good at coming up with ideas that prevent me from feeling the discomfort of my present reality. Yay me!

In the process of writing this chapter, our daughter was hospitalized for anxiety and depression again. At the tender age of 13, I cannot stomach the idea that our little girl has to undergo so much. After an 8-day hunger strike, our daughter reported that the staff would be inserting a feeding tube in her in order to provide her body with some nutrition. As you might imagine, the pain and discomfort I am currently sitting in is overwhelming. While we visited her, we supported her fully and listened to her distorted thinking without judgment. We were present with her. We were in the dark hole with her. As my husband and I got into the car after our visit, I blurted out that I will start looking into different schools for her when she gets out of the hospital. I took off running into the future of when our daughter would return home. I placed myself in that future vision of her going to a great school with loads of support and nice children who wouldn't treat her differently and a program that would address her emotional needs. With one sentence, my husband brought me crashing back to the present moment. "I'm just thinking about how our daughter hasn't eaten in 8 days." It was a good point. It was direct. It was stating reality. It was focused on the present moment. And it hurt. A lot.

Serendipity would have me believe that this chapter of the book came at the right time. Whether it's divine intervention or simply coincidence, I can think of no other example that speaks to the tendency to slip away from the present and into the seductive utopia of the future. I know I have this tendency, yet I'm still surprised when I find myself doing it without even thinking. We, humans, don't do well with discomfort, so I can give myself a break for being human. It makes sense that our minds will look for an escape(s). If you are an outside the box thinker, like me, then maybe you too find yourself using the future as an escape.

Awareness of the urge to futurize is one of many ways to keep an eye on my thinking. I also use deep breathing, sitting in stillness, petting the cat, working out really hard and writing to bring me back to the present. The way we get back to the present isn't as important as the acknowledgment that we need to do it. The present is full of all sorts of joys and delicious life morsels that we miss if we are somewhere other than this moment right now. Yes, the present can be full of discomfort, but running away from it doesn't make it disappear. I've found that being present to the emotions and allowing them to float to the surface has been the key to managing them. Yep it hurts. Yep I cry in public. Yep I still eat Nutella from the jar. But I can shake off the discomfort faster and am less anxious about the next painful moment because I know I can handle it. Just like a pushup, it hurts when I'm doing it but I'm stronger afterward.

Be Present to Be at MOC

In Chapter 7, I talked about being at our Maximum Operating Capacity (MOC), which is when we showcase our strengths, live in alignment with who we are and make decisions based on what is important to us. I've learned that being present allows me to be at my MOC. Even when I have Nutella smeared on my face and my eyes are bloodshot and swollen, I can quickly switch to a moment of joy when I hear my daughter's guinea pigs wheeking or watch the sun rising over the lake or feel the warmth of my fireplace on a cold autumn day. Being present means feeling it all, ALL the time, AT the time. This puts us at our MOC, because we aren't distracted by the past or the future. We are here and now.

An acquaintance of mine, we'll call her Ann, owns a local art business and works for a large security corporation. She uses the corporate gig for income and the local business to express her passion. She was sharing with me during a coaching conversation that her life had become unbearable. She was feeling like she was being crushed by the weight of her soul sucking day job coupled with the poor performance of her local business. Ann was squarely focused on her future debts, like mortgages, university tuitions and retirement savings. She couldn't imagine how she'd be able to afford these items with a failing business and staying in a job she abhors. When I asked her how long she could last if she no longer had any income, her response was "not one day". I challenged her belief that she couldn't last one day without a paycheck. After reflecting on her finances, she reported that she did have millions of dollars tucked away in investments, but it was for the future. It was as if she couldn't see the present reality because she was too busy looking out over the horizon. She had inadvertently placed herself in a dark hole by fixating solely on her future budgetary needs. While I would never advocate that we ignore our future needs, I would also not advocate excluding our current ones. Ann was not taking care of herself physically, emotionally or spiritually, so she of little good to her family, friends, employees and community. On an MOC scale of 1 to 10 with 10 being high, Ann was at a 1 or 2. She wasn't practicing her strengths. Most of her daily work was not in alignment with her values. She spent a majority of her time dealing with issues that were totally unimportant to her. To the outside observer, all of this pain was caused by not living in the present. Ann had missed out on the plethora of joyful moments.

If you are a big, bold thinker, it's easy to think about the "I'll be happy when..." scenarios. For instance, I'll be happy when my daughter gets out the hospital, we have enough money saved up for college or I can buy that adorable little sports car. Here's the big secret. I can be happy right now. Even though my daughter is hurting, we don't have enough money saved for our kids' tuitions, and I drive a 10-year-old SUV, I am at my MOC because I am present to what is happening right now. Being present has freed me to be able to shift my mindset quickly. Having an agile approach makes me more adaptable and better able to discover multiple moments of unexpected enjoyment each day. These little joy titbits have carried me through the most difficult times.

SELF REFLECTIONS

1. How much time do you spend imagining how great it'd be if...?

2. How do you know if you have accepted reality?

3. When you get drawn into the possibilities about the future, how do you bring yourself back to the present moment?

CHAPTER FOURTEEN.
ENGAGE TO LEAD

*"If your actions inspire others to dream more, learn more,
do more and become more, you are a leader."*

JOHN QUINCY ADAMS

O
ne of the things that makes it possible for us different thinkers and lovers of big ideas is our ability to engage people. By drumming up support and resources for our visions, we can experience major follow through for ourselves and others. What I have learned is that impactful engagement includes vulnerability, being present and withholding judgment. It means honoring differences, being flexible and seeking the truth in someone else. It's a lovely place to come from, and people are genuinely drawn to folks who can engage them.

Likeminded People

When you don't think like everyone else in the room, it can be a lonely place. I found that to be true for me, especially after I stopped running from who I am. While I was surrounded by people, I still felt lonely because I didn't feel a deep connection with most people. When I did find another person like me, it was like taking a deep breath after being underwater for too long. In order for me enjoy this sensation, I found that I had to keep an open and curious mind.

I have a client who actually found me by looking for likeminded people. He had outgrown his current group of friends, and he was on a quest to find a new tribe. He had big ideas that he wanted to talk about, and most people would roll their eyes, share their opinions about why his ideas wouldn't work or encourage him to go back to his day job. When he contacted me, I shared with him that I was on a similar journey, so I decided to create a Cross Pollinator dinner. I invited remarkable people from my community, many of whom I didn't know well but heard about them from others, to come to dinner and cross pollinate with each other. My filter was that these folks had to be doing something kick-ass in their business AND in the community. Because of this filter, we discovered that we are all similar in the way we think, and we hit it off immediately. Each idea we toss up is met with wide eyes, smiles and nods of understanding. We have continued this tradition and now meet on a bimonthly basis.

When I invited this person yearning for connection with likeminded people to join us for dinner, he jumped at the chance. The possibility of meeting other big thinkers who wanted to reveal novel ideas, elevate their visions and support each other felt too good to be true for him. Not only did he love the dinner and felt his heart was full when he left, he became a client because he felt like I could understand him as a fellow different thinker.

Digital Engagement

The beauty of today's digital connectivity is that we can locate and connect with likeminded people easily. Social media, in particular, gives us a platform for sharing our big ideas. We can lurk on these sites to see who is doing what. We can lead a mission and see who wants to follow us. We can share our thoughts on certain subjects and see if there are other kindred spirits.

After working with a social media consultant, I discovered a way to create a system to write my big ideas and expose them through social media. Before working with her, I would write anything that came to mind all willy nilly. After our work together, I wrote about beliefs on Mondays, messages on Wednesdays and case studies on Fridays. Each week I would pick one topic to cycle through the three days. It sounds so simple now, but it took some deep inner work to get to this system. This system allowed me to stay focused, have a goal, and write from my heart. Some posts get liked, some get comments and some don't get anything at all. I do know that people like me are enjoying them, and they are finding me through my consistent writing. They reach out to me. They call me. They stop me in town to tell me how much they enjoy my musings. They engage me in deep conversations. They ask me to lead different initiatives, to sit on boards and volunteer for their causes. It is when I stopped hiding and shared on myself that all the good stuff started happening.

Being Vulnerable to Find Your People

As I continue on this journey to find "my" people, I have discovered that vulnerability is closely tied to success. As a recovering hider of who I am, I have to remove my mask(s) to show "my" people who I am. This is scary, regardless of who you are. We all wear different personas, because we are human and it's appropriate at times to protect or hide ourselves. As I become more and more vulnerable, I am experiencing a deeper level of engagement quickly and with more frequency.

As I mention in the Introduction of this book, I was in London on a business trip and experienced a very memorable moment of sheer joy when a stray beagle came up and licked my face in a park on a sunny day as I lay in the grass. The act of laying down is a way of surrendering and making myself vulnerable. Feeling the soft earth beneath my body, enjoying the warmth of the sun on my face and listening to the wind through the leaves on the trees are all ways that I was truly present in that moment. I held no preconceived notions about what might happen. I didn't have any judgments about the day or the people or even the dogs. By being both present and vulnerable, I experienced this exquisite act of love and affection from a four-legged passerby. I have decided to make this mean that I have to be vulnerable and present in order to be engaged.

Switch the Filter

Here is another change that occurred when I stopped running from who I am. When I was desperate for belonging, my focus was always on them. How could I fit in? What did I have to do? What were they looking for? I remember the day when I decided that I should be playing the opposite game. Just switch "I" and "they". How could they fit in? What did they have to do? What was I looking for?

Several years ago, I was in my therapist's office discussing how I was so hungry for love and acceptance from my family. I had tried for years to break in, and yet I always seemed to get pushed outside of the circle. My therapist said these words that I'll never forget. "Allison, you can belong to their group anytime you want. You are a smart woman. You know how to fit in. Right? So go do what you have to do to fit in." She paused and watched as my mind churned with what I would have to do to fit in with them. And I hated it! I didn't want to become that person. From that day forward, I started to evaluate whether or not people fit with me rather than the other way around. I now accept that I will never belong with my family. There is no pain or sadness associated with this fact. Instead, I can actually love them more because I no longer have the resentment of being rejected by them. I have released the need to be a part of that tribe which gave me the freedom to go out and create my own.

Just Like Me

In an effort to build my business recognition, I set about to do presentations and workshops with anyone who'd have me, like networking groups, women's groups, business groups, and university groups. I had to find a way to engage the audience so as to not bore them to tears, as well as appeal to them in case any of my ideal clients were there. Of course, the coach in me would prefer to sit in a circle with the audience and have a really deep conversation rather than yammer at them from a podium. However, that freaks out most people, and it isn't appropriate in many groups. So I have other ways to draw in the audience members and allow them to lower their masks, if only for a brief moment.

I was asked to give a talk to a group of university business students. I was really looking forward to it, and I figured these kids would be easy to motivate, to get talking. Unfortunately, I guess I forgot how much college kids still worry about what others think of them. As I began my talk, I saw very little engagement from these students, like not meeting my eyes and sitting in a slumped position that said, "I don't really want to be here." My talk was about barriers for entrepreneurs, so I presented the first barrier and asked if any of them felt like they have this barrier too. Blank stares. Crickets. So I waited a minute, then raised my hand with great gusto and said, "Just like me." Then some hands went up. I asked them to look around the room to see that we are not alone. I kept on in similar fashion to the fourth and final barrier, and by that point all the students were raising their hands and simultaneously looking around hopefully and then with relief when they saw their peers had the same challenges. I left them a challenge to find a way to support each other, because as they saw in real time, they are all struggling with similar issues. Why not band together and travel that journey together?

Leaders Must Engage

Leadership is one of those things that everybody says they want but nobody can really define. It has become a bit of a sales gimmick, which is too bad because I believe that leaders can change the world. Since I already have a bee in my bonnet about the way the term "leadership" is used excessively, I am sensitive to when I see what I consider to be true leadership. I find that one of the tenets of leadership is the ability to engage people at an intense level.

I had the opportunity to be on a leadership team with a group of coaches putting on a 3-day coaching event for about 150 attendees. I have been on many leadership teams before, but this one was really different. From the beginning, the team leaders engaged us in our intentions. We were given the opportunity to share our own visions for the event with each other. They had taken a vague concept, like setting an intention, and built a clear structure around it. In this way, each leader on the team was wholly engaged not just with their own intention, but also with those of their fellow team members. Additionally, during and after the event, we had several debriefing conversations where we were given the opportunity to cement our learnings and discoveries.

It was with this group that I learned the distinctions between flattery, complimenting and acknowledging. Flattery is given to someone so they will do something for you. Think Erin Brockovich flirting with the water records clerk in order to get files from him. Complimenting is a social nicety but isn't terribly meaningful, like, "I love your shoes." Acknowledging is where it's at. With an acknowledgment, you are sharing who this person is being in the world which comes from a place of compassionate observation and understanding. It means digging below the surface and drawing out the essence of a person. It's a powerful skill and becomes incredibly engaging.

The team leader for this coaching event wrote each of us a letter near the end of the event acknowledging what he witnessed. Below is a copy of what he shared with me.

> *Allison - I acknowledge your tenderness, your delicateness, and your strength. Thank you for creating your strength in such a way that it helped you get through all of the hardships that life has handed you, and thank you for recognizing that you're now ready for a new season — a new harvest. Thank you for practicing letting go of that strength so that the whole truth of who you are can flow into the world.*

This meant so much more to me than a pat on the back, a "nice job", or a thank you card. When I returned home, I felt inspired to write a similar acknowledgment to my school board members, as I am the current president and we are entering into the long and arduous process of searching for a new superintendent. I was hoping that that it would land with them the way it landed with me. I wanted them to know that I see them, know them and understand them. They were so touched, and I feel a much closer connection to each of them as a result. First, because I had to really think about each one of them deeply in order to write the acknowledgment, and second because they got to see who they are in the world to me.

Give 'Em What They Want

Since I started approaching the world looking for people who fit me, I've experienced a shift in my coaching programs. Instead of the plain, old vanilla style coaching agreement with X number of sessions per month, for Y amount of minutes, lasting Z amount of months, I have upped my game. In order to engage my clients more fully, I design each proposal around what I think they would need, which has brought in a whole new element of experiential learning. When I was an engineer, I loved simulations. I could change the variables, run the program and see the results. Likewise, with my clients, I change their variables with real life experiences and then we see what discoveries are made. I am able to honor my client's differences and remain open to the types of experiences that might transform their lives.

For example, I have a client who is already steeped in self-awareness. In the coaching world, we would define him as highly evolved. When I pondered how coaching conversations could further build upon his self-awareness, I felt bored and uninspired. I knew he needed more, but more of what? As I reflected on our past conversations, he shared several times he really enjoyed his experience of working with children. In fact, he mentioned a goal of wanting to work with disadvantaged kids maybe through volunteering or coaching sports. Eureka! Why not include some experiences with at-risk kids where he would have to stretch himself? I built into the proposal field trips to work with different aged, at-risk children.

For another client, we were concluding our 8-month program and discussing what was next. I could tell that he was no longer interested in the standard coaching sessions that had brought him high value only a few months prior. He was looking for something different and he wanted to include his employees. So I crafted a gap analysis for him where I interview him and several of his coworkers to determine the gaps between how he perceives his leadership and how other perceive him. This would give him a working model of where his next level of growth can begin. I also built out a series of group coaching retreats for the entire team to experience deep dives into personal development paired with opportunities to be in nature. Lastly, I have proposed that he also consider being one of four people I will be bringing to Liberia for a leadership program. These highly engaging proposals usually leave my clients salivating.

When I am able to realize my gift of knowing what people need and then finding ways to get those needs met, I find myself full of energy and possibility. I envision my client and me going to an event, kayaking on my lake or leading a group of cranky teens through an exercise that has them cracking a smile and learning about themselves. When I present my proposals to my clients, they're right there with me because the work speaks to what their heart, gut and soul truly want. It's hard not to be excited to work with someone who is so engaged in their growth that has them smiling, clapping their hands and sitting on the edge of their seat.

My level of engagement is transforming their lives. It is creating a pathway for likeminded people to find each other, come together and go after their wants and dreams. It requires me to be open. I have to be curious. I have to find something to like in everyone I meet. I have to be flexible, vulnerable and present. And I have to know who I am, too. I can't help but imagine what the world would be like if more of us would be willing to step forward and find ways to come together.

SELF REFLECTIONS

1. What can being more vulnerable with others do for you?

2. What is your filter for the people you choose to surround yourself with?

3. How can you acknowledge people in your life for who they are in the world?

ACKNOWLEDGEMENTS

'd like to acknowledge Rich Litvin, my coach and mentor, because it is his fault that I wrote this book. Seriously though, it was during a powerful conversation with Rich where he remarked that I had all the makings for a great book on leadership. After that conversation, he posted a fake book cover with my name on Facebook, and I immediately wanted it to be real. This book is the result of that inspiration.

Once I decided to write the book, I felt as though I'd dropped out of a plane on a deserted island with no tools to survive. When I found Ruth Klein, my amazing book coach, I knew she could show me the way. Yes, she has very effective systems and frameworks for writing and marketing books, but I am most thankful for her ability to believe in me more than I believe in myself. Ruth never stops showing me how capable I am.

With the manuscript completed, I was introduced to Giora Litvak who graciously agreed to edit my book. He was brilliant at understanding my voice and suggesting more powerful ways to make my points. He, too, believed in this book and in me, and for that I am truly grateful.

With all the makings of a publishable book, I was introduced to Morgan James Publishing. When they accepted my manuscript, I felt that I was in very good hands. They have moved at the speed I wish, and they have provided me with the resources, knowledge, and support I crave as a first-time author.

Finally, I want to thank my wonderful husband and two teenage children. My family is my foundation, and they never wavered in their ability to support and care for me as I went through this process. I am responsible for lots of things in our family dynamic, and they shifted and filled in when I needed to step away and work on the book. I am forever thankful for the love they so generously give to me.

ABOUT THE AUTHOR

Allison Garner is a coach, consultant, engineer, and author. She has a Bachelor's in Chemical Engineering, Master's in Business Administration, and is a Certified and Credentialed Professional Coach. After serving as an engineer for 20 years in the oil industry with her last position as Vice President of an engineering consulting firm and one of the world's experts in aromatics extraction, she founded her own coaching and consulting practice, Align Coaching LLC, in 2015. In addition to sitting on multiple boards and advisory committees, she has been an elected School Board member for 7 years serving as its Treasurer, Vice President, and President. She has been a resident of Oshkosh, WI, since 2000, where she lives on the beautiful inland Lake Winnebago.

Morgan James
Speakers Group

www.TheMorganJamesSpeakersGroup.com

We connect Morgan James published
authors with live and online events
and audiences who will benefit
from their expertise.

Morgan James makes all of our titles available
through the Library for All Charity Organization.

www.LibraryForAll.org